MORRIS L. VENDEN

HOW TO KNOW

God's Will

IN YOUR LIFE

Pacific Press® Publishing Association
Nampa, Idaho
Oshawa, Ontario, Canada

Edited by Marvin Moore
Cover design by Michelle C. Petz
Cover photo copyright © 1995 by PhotoDisc, Inc.
Inside design by Tim Larson

Library of Congress Card Number: 87-42562

ISBN 0-8163-0719-9

00 01 • 12 11 10

Contents

God's Will in Your Life

Would you like to know the future? Do you wish you knew how to make the right choice in the decisions you face? Do you believe that God has a plan for your life, and do you know how to discover what His plan includes?

The world is full of the search to find out what is coming, stumbling over itself seeking for guidance. The astrology charts are in print on every hand. Fortune tellers and palm readers still abound. People everywhere want to know what will happen next and how to prepare for it. It is part and parcel of being human, this drive and curiosity to find out about tomorrow.

For the Christian, one of the most-often asked questions is how to know God's will in his life. Sometimes we are frustrated by the apparent lack of divine guidance in our day and age. We look back to Bible times, when angels came and walked with men at midday, when prophets were alive and well, and we wish we had the same access to knowing God's will.

On one hand, the immature Christian often resorts to gimmicks and man-made maneuvers, such as flipping a coin or drawing straws or setting up some elaborate routine for God to follow, to make known His will. The guidance received from such methods can come from chance, or even from the devil himself. Even the atheist could employ coins and straws in an attempt to arrive at some decision.

On the other hand, the intellectual Christian concludes that God gave us all the guidance He intended to give when He created us with minds that can think and reason. The Sadducees in the days of Christ were victims of this philosophy and concluded that after starting man in his existence, God left him to his own devices. They believed that the method by which mankind could know God's will for his life was by the simple process of thinking it through and making an arbitrary decision. But once again, if logic and reason contained the whole of God's method for communicating His will, the atheist and infidel could be as certain of making the right choice as could the Christian, and guidance would become a matter of I.Q., rather than spiritual insight.

Perhaps all of us have used one of these approaches at some time in our lives, either concluding that whatever we decide must be God's decision too or trying one of the gimmicks for want of a better method.

One year in college I was faced with a decision concerning my summer employment. This particular summer, I was going to sell books. After writing some letters of inquiry to the various places I could go, I ended up with three invitations: to Washington, Texas, and Wyoming.

It seemed to me that one of the three choices ought to be better, or even the best of the three, and so I wanted God's guidance in order to make the right decision. After considering how this might be done, I decided on a rather sophisticated method. I got out a stack of paper, tore it up into small pieces, and then divided the pieces equally among four stacks. Then I wrote "Washington" on one stack of papers, "Texas" on another stack, and "Wyoming" on the third stack. The fourth stack of papers I left blank, just to be fair to God and give Him the option of "none of the above." You'll have to admit that this was a carefully planned operation!

Then I put all of the pieces of paper in a hat and shook it up and down to mix the pieces. After that, I knelt down and prayed that God would guide me in the decision I was going to make and that if I was supposed to go to one of these three places, or to some unknown place, He would let me know His will by causing me to draw out the same answer three times in a row.

I drew out a slip of paper. It said "Wyoming." I put that slip of paper back, shook the hat some more, and took out a second slip. "Wyoming." I was beginning to get excited! I replaced the second slip, shook the hat one more time, and picked a third slip. "Wyoming"! Three times in a row!

I was elated! I was ready to go out and buy my cowboy boots and Stetson hat that very night! But since it was too late to go shopping, I did the next best thing and rushed across campus to the home of my favorite Bible teacher to tell him the good news.

To my astonishment, he clouded up and rained all over me! He really let me have it. He told me that this was a very immature way to discover God's will, and by the time he had finished, I was no longer elated. My chin dragged all the way back across campus, and I went to sleep that night a very discouraged student.

But I still had to make the decision. During the next day, I began to think about Gideon. Now there's a Bible example for you—good old Gideon! He asked God for a sign, not once, but twice. And God honored his request by causing the fleece to be first wet, then dry. The more I thought about Gideon, the more I was sure that my Bible teacher didn't know everything after all!

So that evening I reminded the Lord of Gideon and got my hat out for the second time around. I shook it thoroughly and once again drew out three slips of paper. "Wyoming," "Wyoming," and "Wyoming"—three times in a row the second night as well.

Now I was excited again! I took off across campus—but not to the same Bible teacher's house! He obviously hadn't appreciated the miracle that was taking place, so I decided to try someone else. I chose another Bible teacher this time and told him about what had happened—two evenings in a row.

He was no more encouraging than the first teacher had been. He also reproved me for my immature methods and suggested that there was no guarantee that God would choose to communicate through the system that I had set up.

So I threw away the pieces of paper, and that summer I ended up going to Nebraska! I've often wondered what would have happened if I had gone to Wyoming.

Actually, I am not willing to throw this experience out entirely. God often meets people where they *are* and graciously responds to their seeking after Him, even when they do not understand that much about Him. But perhaps the greatest lesson I received from the Lord in this experience was a better understanding of how to seek His guidance, according to what His Word reveals as the best methods for seeking Him!

If you have ever read biographies of George Mueller, you know that his track record for understanding the Lord's guidance was impressive. For the first twenty years of his life Mueller was a reprobate. After his conversion, he began a ministry that was to last more than fifty years, running orphanages for the street urchins of Bristol. He never had a public relations man. He never advertised his needs. Whenever he needed money, food, or clothes for his orphans, he told no one, but went to his closet and prayed. During his lifetime, George Mueller received millions of dollars solely in answer to prayer.

One time Mueller was on a ship out in the Atlantic, headed for Bristol. Fog came in, and the captain of the ship who later told the story had been at his post for three days, guiding the ship at a snail's pace. Mueller approached him and said, "Captain, I need to be in Bristol on Saturday."

"There's no way you'll be in Bristol on Saturday," the captain replied. "Can't you see this fog?"

Mueller replied, "My eyes are not on the fog, but on the living God. Captain, will you go below with me and pray that God will remove the fog?"

The captain followed Mueller below, and they knelt together. Mueller said a simple prayer that a Sunday School boy might have prayed. "Dear Jesus, You know about the appointment that You made for me in Bristol on Saturday, so please take the fog away. Amen."

The captain was going to try to manufacture some kind of prayer, but Mueller stopped him. "In the first place, you don't believe God can do it," he said, "and in the second place, I believe He's already done it. If you will go back up to the bridge, you will find that the fog is gone."

The captain went outside and discovered that the fog was indeed gone, just as Mueller had said. They were in Bristol on Saturday.

How is it possible to be so sure of God's will? How could Mueller live with such certainty? When someone who is that tuned in to the will of the Lord begins sharing with you how to know God's will, you listen. Near the close of his godly life, Mueller gave seven steps for knowing God's will. I checked these out in the inspired material on the

subject and added one more. I would like to invite you to
study these steps and make use of them in your own life.
We will list the eight points and then consider them in
greater detail in each of the next eight chapters.

1. *No will of your own on the given matter.* Your own
will is in neutral. This does not mean you will have no
preference, but that you are willing to go in whatever
way God directs. This is only possible for one who is involved in daily fellowship with God, for we cannot bring
ourselves to surrender. God must do that for us. Jesus'
example in this is recorded in Matthew 26:39 and John
4:34.

2. *Don't go simply by feeling.* In fact, you don't go by any
one single step. It is the combination of all eight of them
together that is significant. But often there is the temptation to make your decision on the basis of feelings, so this
is a warning. Don't do it! Although the Holy Spirit often
leads through impressions upon the heart (see Isaiah
30:21), we should never make a decision on the basis of
feelings alone.

3. *Study God's Word* to see what is revealed that may
give direction on the present decision. God always guides
us through His Word, never contrary to it. See Psalm
119:105. There may not be specific *information* on your
particular decision, although there are often principles
that apply. But you can always go to the Word for *communication.*

4. *Consider providential circumstances.* "Thou shalt remember all the way which the Lord thy God led thee."
Deuteronomy 8:2. Look at God's leading in the past and
see how the current decision might fit into a pattern that
has already been developing.

5. *Consult with godly friends.* This is the step that I
added to Mueller's list. It's found in Proverbs 11:14 and

Psalm 1:1. Don't consult with your *un*godly friends! And once again, don't make your entire decision based on what your friends say. But put their counsel into your portfolio to help you come to a decision.

6. *Ask God, in prayer, to reveal His will* to you concerning the decision you are going to make. See James 1:5.

7. *Make a decision!* On the basis of what has gone before, in the first six steps, make a decision. Don't wait for a sign or a bolt of lightning from heaven. Consider prayerfully the weight of evidence, and decide. And tell God what your decision is.

8. *Proceed with your decision*, inviting God to stop you if you have missed your signals. Then be sensitive to the swinging doors. God knows how to open and close doors. At times, you may find a door slammed in your face. I've had it happen on occasions! And it's usually because I've missed it on step one. But even the apostle Paul found doors closing in his face at times. You can read about it in Acts 16:6-9.

Those are the steps, and for those of us who have used them over the years in making decisions and in seeking to know God's will in those decisions, we have found that they are extremely helpful.

God has a will. He is interested in guiding you in the decisions of your life. He has a plan for you, and your greatest happiness will be found in following that plan. If it is His will for you to go to Nineveh, it will not be equally satisfactory for you to head for Tarshish. God knows what will be best for you and bring the greatest blessing to others, and He is willing to make His will known to those who are willing to listen.

In Psalm 32:8 the promise is given, "I will instruct thee and teach thee in the way which thou shalt go: I will guide thee with mine eye." John 10:3-5 says, "The sheep hear his voice; and he calleth his own sheep by name, and leadeth them out. And when he putteth forth his own sheep, he goeth before them, and the sheep follow him: for they know his voice. And a stranger will they not follow, but will flee from him: for they know not the voice of strangers."

David prayed, "Lead me in the way everlasting." Psalm 139:24. Proverbs 3:5, 6 says, "Trust in the Lord with all thine heart; and lean not unto thine own understanding. In all thy ways acknowledge him, and he shall direct thy paths." Paul tells us in Romans 12:2, "Be not conformed to this world: but be ye transformed by the renewing of your mind, that ye may prove what is that good, and acceptable, and perfect, will of God." And Jeremiah 10:23 says, "O Lord, I know that the way of man is not in himself: it is not in man that walketh to direct his steps."

We could list many other Bible references to prove the point. God wants to lead us, to guide us, to manifest Himself to us. He does not desire that we rely upon our own feeble wisdom, nor that we stumble about in the dark, not knowing whether or not we are choosing aright. He has a will, and He wants to reveal that will to us.

But there is a major premise to understanding God's will that we want to underline and emphasize before we go any further. For the one who truly is seeking to know God's will, there will be a daily seeking to know God. The matter of guidance is not a fire escape routine, that calls upon God only when there is a major decision to be faced. It is in seeking to know God day by day, through prayer and the study of His Word, that we are brought into a position to even begin to know His will in regard to the details of our daily lives.

Suppose I were to give you a list of steps to use in learning how to swim. Suppose, furthermore, you were to go down through the list holding your breath, moving your arms, cupping your hands, and kicking your feet. Suppose that finally you came back to me and said, "It didn't work! I still can't swim." And as we discuss the difficulty, we discover that you never realized you were supposed to be *in the water!* That would represent a serious breakdown in communication, wouldn't it?

It would be a tragedy to make the same mistake here, in the arena of knowing God's will in your life. I cannot emphasize it too much, elementary as it is. *In order to know God's will in your life, you must first know God.* It is not enough only to turn to Him when there is a problem or crisis.

Notice again the verses in John 10. It is the sheep who know His voice, who are able to follow the leading of the Shepherd. They have become familiar enough with the Shepherd that they can distinguish His voice from all the other voices. Then, when He speaks, they can follow His guidance.

Do you know Him? Do you know what it means to set aside prime time each day to further your acquaintance and relationship with Him? Do you know what it means to talk to Him, just for the sake of talking, even when you don't need anything from Him but Himself? Do you know what it means to listen to Him talk to you, through His Word? Have you experienced, as the disciples did on the road to Emmaus, what it is like to have your heart burn within you as He talks with you by the way? Are you on speaking terms with Him day by day?

If you can answer Yes to these questions, then you are in a position to seek His guidance with regard to the particular details of your life. If you do not know Him, then your first work is to become acquainted with Him for yourself. It is only when you know Him for yourself that you can correctly understand His guidance, or even be willing to accept His guidance when it is understood.

Don't try to learn to swim by the method described in the old nursery rhyme:

Mother, may I go out to swim?
Yes, my darling daughter.
Hang your clothes on the hickory limb,
But don't go near the water!

Get in the water! Become acquainted with the best Friend you can ever have. Learn to know Him. And then as you face the decisions of life, you can learn to know His will for you in your daily living as well.

Step 1
God's Will and Your Will

Perhaps we know him best because of his donkey. Although Balaam was a prophet of God for a time, in the end he proved false. He missed the right understanding and acceptance of God's will in his life because he was unwilling to give up his own plans. And his life ended in tragedy.

You remember the story. The children of Israel had come to the borders of the Promised Land. Balak, the Moabite king, was immediately concerned. The Israelites, camped across the Jordan River on the plains of Moab, represented a mighty force, and Balak wasn't sure that his army was equal to theirs. So he decided to try some strategy.

He sent messengers to Balaam, saying, "Behold, there is a people come out from Egypt: behold, they cover the face of the earth, and they abide over against me: Come now therefore, I pray thee, curse me this people; for they are too mighty for me: peradventure I shall prevail, that we may smite them, and that I may drive them out of the land: for I wot that he whom thou blessest is blessed, and he whom thou cursest is cursed." Numbers 22:5, 6.

It might seem at first glance that Balaam should have known right away that this was not God's plan! But he was so impressed by the rewards the king offered for his services that he said to the messengers, "Lodge here this night, and I will bring you word again, as the Lord shall speak unto me." Verse 8. And so the messengers stayed there overnight.

Balaam asked for guidance, and the guidance of the Lord came back loud and clear. "God said unto Balaam, Thou shalt not go with them; thou shalt not curse the people: for they are blessed." Verse 12.

Balaam reluctantly sent the messengers on their way the next morning, and they returned to Balak with the message. But Balak wasn't so easily discouraged. He sent back a second group of messengers who promised greater rewards than the first time, concluding that Balaam was simply holding out for a higher price. He promised honor and promotions for Balaam, if Balaam would cooperate with his plan.

Balaam's words were right, for he replied, in verse 18, "If Balak would give me his house full of silver and gold, I cannot go beyond the word of the Lord my God, to do less or more." But Balaam's heart was not right. His own will was set—he wanted desperately to go with the messengers, speak the required curses against Israel, and receive the reward. Perhaps he reasoned that words are nothing anyway, that God's people could not be hurt by his incantations, and his own case would very obviously be helped. Surely he had rationalizations that he rehearsed in his mind, as he once again went before the Lord to inquire about His will in the matter.

God was very patient with this erring prophet and came and spoke to him once more. He said, "If the men come to call thee, rise up, and go with them." Verse 20.

Balaam didn't ask for a sign, so far as we know, but the Lord offered him one. "If they come and call for you, go with them. If not, stay home." But the messengers didn't come to call for Balaam. Impatient at the delay, and expecting the same reply as before, they didn't suppose anything was to be gained by waiting around. Early in the morning, they went on their way, and by the time Balaam went to look for them, they had already left to return to the palace.

Balaam's own will was in complete control by this time, and, ignoring the direct command of the Lord, he saddled his donkey and went after the messengers. Before he caught up with them, he was interrupted by the angel—invisible to him in the beginning, but seen by his donkey. Balaam's mind was made up. He knew what *he* wanted. And even a talking donkey and an angel with a drawn sword were not enough to change his mind. He didn't stop because he was willing to stop. He stopped because he was forced to stop. He said to the angel, "Now therefore, if it displease thee, I will get me back again." It would seem that Balaam had been given one or two clues about whether or not God was displeased with his course of action, wouldn't it? But Balaam was determined to go ahead if there was any way he could manage to do it.

God, in His infinite regard for man's power of choice, allowed Balaam his own way, but told him he could speak only the words given him by God.

It's easy to join Balaam, isn't it? It is not difficult to understand God's will when it is in harmony with our own inclinations. But when we see that the will of the Lord would lead us in some way other than what we would choose for ourselves, how hard we find it to hear His voice! We may pray long and earnestly, asking God to show us what we should do, but God knows our hearts. He knows whether we are sincere in seeking to know His will or whether we are simply seeking His stamp of approval on our own choice. He may sometimes deal with us as He did with Balaam and allow us to go ahead in the path we have chosen, until we come to realize that we have not given up our own will in the matter. For it is only when we have no will of our own that we are in a position to begin seeking for the will of the Lord.

Balaam and Balak tried three times to curse Israel, but Balaam could speak only blessings. Balak finally lost his temper and said, "I called thee to curse mine enemies, and, behold, thou hast altogether blessed them these three times." Numbers 24:10. Balaam headed for home, shouting blessings on Israel over his shoulder as he left, and with anger in his heart for being cheated out of the riches and honors that should have been his had he been able to provide curses instead of blessings.

After he reached his home, he came up with another plan for cursing Israel. Without even consulting the Lord this time, for he knew he was in rebellion, he returned to the palace with a clever idea. He knew the source of Israel's strength, even if Balak did not. And he also knew that when God's people were separated from the source of their strength, the curse would be automatic.

Balak was delighted with Balaam's plan and immediately put it into action. Balaam was given the honor and riches that he so coveted, but he did not enjoy them for very long, for he was slain in the battle that followed.

Balaam is a classic example of the truth of the first step in seeking to know God's will in your life. You must have *no will of your own in the given matter.* If your own will is in control, it will be of no value to you to know the will of God, for you won't be willing to accept it. If your own will is in control, even the voice of God in the night or a talking donkey or an angel blocking your pathway or your own judgment and reason and conscience, will not be sufficient to turn you from your course. Your own will must be given into the control of God before a revelation of His will for you would be accepted and appreciated.

What does it mean to have no will of your own? Suppose you are trying to decide whom to marry or where to move or what job to accept. Does having no will of your own mean that you have no preference in the matter? Does having no will of your own make you some kind of marshmallow, with no thought or desire about what you want?

Having no will of your own does *not* mean that you will have no preference. Jesus had a preference in the Garden of Gethsemane, when He prayed, "Not my will, but thine, be done." Luke 22:42. He would have preferred to escape the agonies of the Garden, the humiliation of the public trial, the scourgings, and the horror of the cross. He would have preferred not to be separated from His Father. He had a preference. But greater than His personal preference was His commitment to bring salvation to this world, to cooperate with His Father in the work of redemption. Therefore, in spite of His own preference, He could say, "I came down from heaven, not to do mine own will, but the will of him that sent me." John 6:38.

So it's one thing to have a preference; it's another thing to be so totally surrendered to whatever God's will for you might be that as soon as His will is revealed, you're willing. To have no will of your own means to have as your first priority to accept His will, so that as soon as His will is revealed, you accept and cherish it, and your own preference is surrendered.

Whenever someone misses the Lord's guidance in his life, it usually comes as a result of missing it on this first step—having no will of your own on the given matter. But it is impossible to come to the place of having no will of your own, apart from a personal relationship with

Christ. Only His power and control in your life can bring you to a genuine surrender to His will. If you are in control of yourself, you will join Balaam every time, saying to God, "My mind is made up; don't confuse me with facts."

There are many Bible examples of those who apparently sought for the guidance of the Lord, but who did not surrender their own wills in the process. The children of Israel, in their first trip to the borders of the Promised Land, less than two years after they left Egypt, made the same mistake. They sent out spies to see what this new land looked like, and when the spies came back with their negative report, the people gave in to fear and doubt. They refused the opportunity to accept God's will for them, that they go in at once and possess the land. Caleb and Joshua pleaded with them in vain. Moses and Aaron were unable to talk them out of their decision. They prayed to die in the wilderness, and their prayer was tragically answered according to their desire.

Saul was unwilling to wait for Samuel to arrive to offer the sacrifices as priest, and went ahead on his own. He was unwilling to accept the Lord's directions regarding the captives and the spoils of war and went his own way instead. He was unwilling, in the end, to even consult God's will, which had so often been in collision with his own, and went instead to the witch of Endor to find more agreeable counsel.

Samson wasn't willing to accept God's guidance for him in choosing a wife. Jezebel wasn't willing to accept the guidance of the Lord through Elijah, and sought to kill him instead. David consulted his own will instead of the will of the Lord in his relationship with Bathsheba. The list could go on and on.

Perhaps our greatest handicap in understanding the

will of the Lord for our lives is our own will being so constantly in the picture. And that is why we have no hope of having no will of our own, except as we come to Christ day by day and surrender to Him on a daily basis, through the ongoing personal relationship with Him. If we surrender to Him day by day, and day by day accept His control in our lives, then when the time comes for decision, we will be in a position to have no will of our own and to accept God's will for us.

Christ, in His life on earth, made no plans for Himself. Day by day He received His Father's plans for Him, and it was thus that His life constantly was in harmony with His Father's will. The same guidance that He had is available to us.

Does this mean that we make no plans at all, that we just sit in a rocking chair and wait for God to rock it? Or does it mean that we make no plans apart from God—no plans for *ourselves* that ignore Him? We may make plans, as best we know, but we must always be willing to give up those plans, or carry them out, as His providence shall indicate.

The apostle Paul is an example of this. In his missionary journeys he made plans, but sometimes his plans were interrupted. Acts 16:6-9 tells about it. They were planning to go one place, but the Holy Spirit directed them instead to another, and they accepted His plans, for they were surrendered to His control. They were willing for their own plans to be interrupted whenever those plans were not in harmony with the plans of God.

You see it at work in the life of Jesus. He and His disciples were near a Samaritan village. Jesus was so tired that He couldn't even walk the rest of the way into town with His disciples, but instead sat by the well, planning to rest until His disciples brought back some food. But

His plans for rest were interrupted. A woman came to draw water from the well, and she was in need of His help. His Father had scheduled a divine appointment, and Jesus accepted the challenge. When His disciples, surprised at His actions, questioned Him concerning them, He replied, "My meat is to do the will of him that sent me, and to finish his work." John 4:34. What does that mean? It means that for the person who is following in the footsteps of Jesus, if there ever comes a choice, even a choice between eating and service, he will know which choice to make. And not only will he know what is the right choice, he will count it a privilege and honor to choose to serve Him.

You may be tired or hungry or thirsty. But the Lord may send you a divine appointment, and when you accept His guidance, you discover strength you didn't know you had. Have you ever had it happen? The Lord may send you to some place of service that you would never have chosen for yourself. But as you follow His guidance, you discover that the greatest blessing comes to you in going where He leads you.

Do you want to have no will of your own? It is possible in only one way. As you continue the relationship with God, seeking Him day by day as your first priority, He will take you to the place of having no will of your own. And at any time you see His directions and pull back from the relationship with Him in order to go your own way, you are in danger.

I knew a young man who did not want to be a minister. Every time he was close to God, he would feel the tap of God on his shoulder, bringing the conviction that God wanted him to be a minister. But he definitely did not want to be a minister. So he found a solution. He stayed an arm's length away from God. He deliberately chose not to get too close. Then he didn't feel the tap!

I read the story one time of a man who was so determined not to become a minister, and so convicted that God wanted him to be one, that he refused to give his heart to the Lord, refused to become converted, refused to come to God for repentance and forgiveness and power. He stayed away for years, until finally one day he gave up the struggle. He said that when that time came, he didn't begin by asking forgiveness for his sins or asking for repentance or for acceptance with God. His first prayer, when he finally allowed God to catch up with him was, "OK, so I'll be a minister." And all the rest of the ingredients for salvation came after that.

For several years our family lived in northern California, at a place that was more like a resort than anything else. It was up in the mountains, quiet, peaceful, beautiful. Then we received a call to go to Nebraska.

We were not interested in going to Nebraska. We didn't want anything to do with Nebraska. We made jokes about getting a bumper sticker that said, "Ski Nebraska." We spoke, tongue-in-cheek, about Nebraska being the recreational capital of the world.

It took quite a while before we were even willing to pray about whether to go to Nebraska. But the time came, in the ongoing relationship with Christ, when it was necessary to either listen to His will about Nebraska or scrap the relationship. So we prayed about the call to Nebraska.

In spite of the length of time it took Him to bring us around to having no will of our own on the given matter, once we were willing to give up our own preference, His will became very clear in an amazingly short time.

When we moved to Nebraska, the reports of our earlier attitude had preceded us! The office at the church had

been decorated with banners that read "Ski Nebraska"—
and other "inside" jokes! We were embarrassed! But we
were also thankful that the people in Nebraska had a
sense of humor!

In the end, not only were we willing to be in Nebraska,
but we were actually excited about the prospect and could
hardly wait to see what God's plan was for us in that
place, since He had been so definite about leading us
there.

Does God have a special place in mind for you to work
for Him? Yes, He does, just as surely as He has a special
place for you prepared in heaven. And no matter what
your personal preferences might be, if you accept His
choice for you in your life, in your home, in your service
for Him, you will find the greatest happiness. And the
first step toward finding that will for your life is to allow
Him to bring you to the point of having *no will of your
own in the given matter.*

Step 2
God's Will and Your Feelings

Suppose you received a check in the mail from some multimillionaire, made out in your name, for the amount of $10,000. You would probably feel pretty excited, wouldn't you? You might feel a little skeptical as well. But you check it out, and sure enough, it is intended for you. You feel elated and show it to your friends and neighbors. You plan how you will spend it or invest it or save it for some future occasion. And finally, the day comes when you are ready to take it to the bank and cash it.

But that day you aren't feeling too well. The excitement has worn off. You're coming down with a cold, and your throat is sore. Perhaps you're feeling a little guilty, realizing that you did nothing to deserve this gift of $10,000. Maybe you still feel like it's too good to be true. But you go down to the bank, and after you stand in line for a few minutes, your turn comes at the window. By this time you're feeling completely miserable. *But you still have $10,000.*

The teller and the bank are not concerned with your feelings. You may be happy or depressed; it makes no difference. The deciding factor as to whether or not the money is yours is based completely on the value of the check and the signature of the person who gave it to you. Your feelings are beside the point.

Step two in learning God's will in your life and understanding His guidance is more of a warning than an actual process. It is that *you don't go by feelings*.

This is a valid warning, because often the temptation is to do just that. Perhaps when you first begin to seek God's will on a subject, you have a "first impression" of what His answer should be. Later on, if His answer is delayed, it is easy to become impatient and discouraged. But you cannot trust either the first impulse, or the waffling back and forth of emotions that can go on in the course of making a particular decision. Feelings are never a safe guide.

The Campus Crusade people have a little diagram that they use to illustrate this point. They picture an engine, a coal car, and a caboose. The engine is labeled fact. The coal car represents faith. And the caboose is called feeling. If you try to run a train by the caboose, you're in trouble. It is the engine that must pull the train. And in the end, the engine can make the trip with or without the caboose.

Feelings can include a lot of territory. Are you afraid to do a particular thing? Does it go against your personal tastes? Does it sound exciting? Do you think it would be fun? Does it seem that you are not qualified for the task? Is this just what you've always wanted? The list could go on and on. Feelings, both good and bad, come in many varieties.

One reason why this second step is so important is that in trying to understand the will of God in your life, it is important to consider all of the eight steps, and not just one or two. The eight steps provide a system of checks and balances. You may miss your signals on one step, but the other steps may show you where you erred. In the end, the decision is made on the basis of the weight of evidence, not on the basis of *any* single step. But the warning is included here under step two because this step is perhaps the one that is easiest to consider complete in itself. It is an important warning because feelings, both positive and negative, can be pretty powerful incentives. Yet if you try to run your spiritual life on the basis of feelings, you will find yourself in as much difficulty as if you tried to run the railroad train by the caboose. It gets you nowhere.

However, we should not disregard feelings completely. One of the methods by which the Lord communicates His will to us is through the impressions of the Holy Spirit upon the heart. Impressions and feelings can seem very much alike, can't they? How do you know the difference between simple feelings, the impulse of the moment, and the conviction of the Spirit in your mind?

Let's recognize first of all that there are some feelings that are sinful and some feelings that are not sinful. Sinful feelings could include fear, lust, doubt, anger, or covetousness. Feelings that are *not* sinful could include things like hope, happiness, weariness, hunger, or sadness.

The devil likes to work through our feelings to lead us away from God. If we are feeling joyful and optimistic, he will try to get us to carry it to extremes and become involved in fanaticism or presumption, running ahead of God. If we are feeling discouraged and sad, he will try to awaken fear and distrust, so that we will give in to his temptations.

You can see this happening in the case of Elijah. He had some very positive feelings on top of Mount Carmel. The end of the three and a half years of famine had come, and with it the showdown between God and Baal. It must have been a tremendous thrill for him when the fire came flashing down from heaven, consuming the sacrifice and the altar and the water around beneath. His *faith* was strong. He believed that God would respond to vindicate His own honor and His name before the people. But what tremendous *feelings* must have surged through him as he stood there and watched it happen!

Then Elijah led out in the judgment upon the 400 prophets of Baal, which was surely a major strain on the nervous system! His heart must have been torn apart with sorrow and horror and agony at the task he was led to perform.

Next he went to the mountaintop and began to pray for rain. The rain didn't come immediately as had the fire from heaven, and Elijah was filled with self-doubt. He stayed there on top of the mountain, searching his heart and continuing to press his petitions until his servant came back and reported a small cloud on the horizon. That's all it took. Elijah rose up and ran before the chariots of Ahab all the way back to the city—the first marathon!

When Elijah went to sleep that night in a quiet corner outside the city walls with his mantle wrapped around him, he must have been as drained emotionally as anyone could be. He was also exhausted physically. His feelings had been torn in shreds all through that long and eventful day. Now the devil moved in to take advantage of feelings that *weren't* sinful, to lead him into feelings that *were*.

Elijah was awakened abruptly and warned that Jezebel was out to take his life. At that point his weariness and hunger and sorrow turned to fear. He crossed the line into the devil's territory. Fear gets bad marks in Scripture. Read it in Revelation 21:8. The fearful are among those who find their place in the lake of fire, along with some pretty sordid bedfellows. In spite of his strong faith that had sustained him earlier in the day, Elijah now gave in to blind panic and set out to save himself. He fled into the desert, abandoning his post of duty, trying to escape from the threats of Jezebel. He was so despondent that he ended up asking that he might die, since he was the only one left in Israel who was true to God. What a contrast between the fearful, running Elijah, and the Elijah on top of Mount Carmel who thundered out to the multitudes, "How long halt ye between two opinions? if the Lord be God, follow him." 1 Kings 18:21.

So one indication as to whether or not your feelings are from the conviction of the Holy Spirit or from your own humanity would be to examine whether or not the feelings are sinful. The Holy Spirit will never lead through sinful feelings, wouldn't that be safe to say? Second Timothy 1:7 says, "God hath not given us the spirit of fear; but of power, and of love, and of a sound mind."

Another aspect to consider, in trying to determine whether or not your feelings are simply feelings, or the impressions of the Holy Spirit upon your heart, is to look at the difference between conviction and guilt. Guilt always comes from the devil. Conviction always comes from the Holy Spirit. At first glance, these two may seem to be very much alike. But guilt always leaves us hopeless and despairing. When the devil beats us over the head with guilt, he is trying to get us to give up and give in, trying to get us to decide that our case is without remedy.

On the other hand, the conviction that comes from the Holy Spirit comes with hope and courage for tomorrow. It never leaves us in despair. The Holy Spirit never leads us to a place of conviction and recognition of our deep need of God's grace, without also leading us beyond that place, to the solution found in the sacrifice of Jesus and His right-eousness to be accepted in our behalf. The Holy Spirit brings conviction, but never condemnation.

Another factor to consider in trying to distinguish between our own feelings and the impressions or convictions of the Holy Spirit is the question of who is in the center of focus. Our feelings may lead us to put our own interests first and focus our attention on what's best for us. The Holy Spirit will lead us to make the glory and honor of God and the needs of those around us the first consideration.

John the Baptist had strong feelings against being in the dungeon of Herod. He was used to the wide open spaces, with freedom to come and go as he pleased. He had been accustomed to an active life. He was no more delighted over being imprisoned in the gloomy dungeon than you or I would have been. If he had put his own needs first, he would have quickly recanted from his stern rebukes and regained his freedom. But he put his own desires aside, for loyalty to God demanded that he speak fearlessly for truth and let God be in charge of the consequences of such faithfulness. He put the glory and honor of God first, and in spite of the loneliness and isolation of his prison life, he was able to keep saying, "He must increase, but I must decrease." John 3:30.

We may sometimes be able to see the difference between our feelings and the impressions of the Holy Spirit by applying the test of reason and judgment. We may be able to reason from cause to effect, to recognize when we are particularly tired or suffering from the effects of extreme stress. And God wants us to exercise good judgment and common sense in the decisions of life.

But reason and judgment may not be enough. Some of the most foolish actions in all the Bible were performed by those who were the most closely under the control of God. How about Gideon, attacking the enemy with pitchers and torches and 300 men? What about Jonathan and his armorbearer taking on a whole army by themselves? What about David, clad in the simple garments of a shepherd boy, going out single-handed to meet the giant Goliath, who was covered with armor from head to toe? Or Joshua, trying to capture a city by walking in circles around it and blowing trumpets?

If we are under God's control and tuned in to His leading in our lives, He may at times lead us to do things that apparently go completely against good judgment and common sense. So although reason and judgment should be considered, they can never be a final proof for or against God's guidance.

We may be able to distinguish between simple feelings and the impressions of the Holy Spirit by giving the test of time. If there is time before the decision must be made, there can be real value in "sleeping on it," in order to allow time for prayer and meditation to determine the source of the impulses. But even the test of time may not be adequate. There may not be time enough to give such a test! What about Phinehas, when Israel was about to cross over into the land of Promise? Balaam's plot for cursing Israel was in full effect, and the rebellion had become so widespread that one of the leaders in Israel came into the camp in broad daylight, accompanied by a Moabite harlot, and took her openly into his tent.

Phinehas, the high priest's son, didn't go home to think it over and make sure he wasn't being impulsive. He went into the tent and pinned them both to the ground with one thrust of his javelin!

Mary Magdalene, that night at Simon's feast, didn't take time to wait till the next day to see if the impulse to anoint Jesus was still around. If she had, the opportunity to anoint Jesus would no longer have been available. When the Holy Spirit prompted Mary to action, she obeyed instantly. She could not explain why she had chosen that occasion for honoring Jesus. When the accusations began, she was speechless. But Jesus recognized her deed of love and made an interesting promise concerning it. He said that wherever the gospel would be told, for as long as time should last, the story of Mary's action would be repeated as well—and here is just one more time.

So there are certain things we can consider when we try to decide whether our feelings are just feelings, or whether they are inspired by the Holy Spirit. We can consider whether they are sinful feelings. We can be aware of the difference between guilt and conviction. We can look at whether the focus is on ourselves or on the honor and glory of God. We can apply the test of reason and judgment—to a point. We can allow for the test of time—when there is time for such a test.

But the greatest help in recognizing the difference between simple feeling and the inner voice of the Spirit is to know God. As we noticed in the last chapter, from John 10, the sheep recognize the voice of the Shepherd and distinguish that voice from the voice of a stranger, because they know Him.

Abraham knew God. He had spent time out under the stars when the rest of his world was asleep, communing with the God of heaven. When God came to him and told him to leave his country and kindred behind and go to some unknown destination, he went forward, because he recognized the voice of God from their previous contact. He didn't go by his feelings. He was guided by what he knew God's directions to be.

At the end of his life, when the time came for the supreme test, he was unable to go by feelings. Everything in his father's heart resisted the command to offer up Isaac as a sacrifice. All of his hopes and dreams, all of the past promises of God, argued against such a plan. But he knew God's voice and, disregarding his feelings, in spite of how strong they were, he again went out according to the word of the Lord.

As you know, Abraham had heard God's voice correctly, and when he had been fully tested, a glorious deliverance was provided, giving a lesson that will speak through all time, and to the entire universe, of the love of God in sending His Son to die in our place.

So when it comes to knowing God's will in our lives, it is important not to decide simply on the basis of feeling. It is important to consider all of the steps to knowing God's guidance. But the greatest assurance, behind all of the methods for knowing that you are following His leading, is to know Him—and He will make it plain to you what His will for you includes. To know Him, and to know His voice, is essential, if we would be certain that we *do not go by simple feelings*.

Step 3

God's Will
and His Word

The third step in trying to understand God's will in your life is to *consult His Word*. Psalm 119:105 tells us, "Thy word is a lamp unto my feet, and a light unto my path." If God leads us at all, He will lead us through His Word, and God will never lead us contrary to His Word.

The Word of God is given as more than just a history lesson. It is more than an account of the lives of people who have long been dead. It is more than prophecy. It is more than doctrine. It is more than genealogy. It is more than a storybook. It is the living Word of God, which liveth and abideth forever.

We can approach the Word of God in two ways: first for information, and second for communication. Is the Word of God a valuable source of information? Of course it is. It gives an accurate account of the history of mankind. It "tells it like it is," candidly recording both the failures and the triumphs of the people of God. It is "given by inspiration of God, and is profitable for doctrine, for reproof, for correction, for instruction in righteousness." 2 Timothy 3:16.

The information in the Word of God can be trusted to be accurate, and through His Word God has given information that He knew would be needed by His people in this world for as long as time would last.

But when you come to the Bible for guidance, there may not be a specific chapter and verse for the decision you are trying to make. Suppose you are trying to decide where to move or what job to accept or whether to marry one person or another. There is nowhere in Scripture where you can find a verse that says, "You are supposed to marry Jim," or, "You should become a doctor." And so we must understand the second purpose of the Word of God: communication.

We might go so far as to say that the *primary* purpose of God's Word is for communication. There is a major difference between knowing about God, and *knowing God*. The apostle Paul considered knowing God to be the most important aspect of life, for he said in Philippians 3:7-10, "But what things were gain to me, those I counted loss for Christ. Yea, doubtless, and I count all things but loss . . . that I may know him." Jeremiah wrote, "Let not the wise man glory in his wisdom, neither let the mighty man glory in his might, let not the rich man glory in his riches: but let him that glorieth glory in this, that he understandeth and knoweth me." Jeremiah 9:23, 24. And Daniel said, "The people that do know their God shall be strong." Daniel 11:32.

Because God's Word must be an avenue of communication, and not just a source of information, we must underscore once again that the basis for learning God's will in your life must always be the personal, daily, ongoing relationship with Him. If you have never known what it means to make use of the Word of God for communication and fellowship with Him, the information to be found there will prove of little benefit. Even if there is information so specific to your situation that you can't miss it, you won't have the spiritual strength to accept His Word

unless you have become personally acquainted with Him.
He must give not only the wisdom, but the power for obedience. It is not enough to know what is right and wrong.
We must also understand how to accept His control so
that we will be able to obey.

But when you have been in fellowship and communion
with God day by day, and the time comes for some decision in your life, you can go to His Word first for information and then for communication with Him where the
specific information is lacking.

Of course it is true that the Bible gives many principles
of life that we can apply toward our specific situation. For
instance, the Bible warns against marriage between un-
believers. If you are choosing between someone whose
spiritual life is compatible with yours and someone who is
uninterested in spiritual things, you have some rather
powerful help in making that kind of a decision. The Bible warns against dishonesty. If you have to lie in order to
get or keep a particular job, you can know on the basis of
Scripture that God is not leading in that direction. So
even though there may not be a specific chapter or verse
for your situation, there may be principles that would apply and help you in making the right decision.

However, there are times when you may be choosing
between two apparently "right" choices, instead of between right and wrong. You may be choosing whether to
become a math teacher or a science teacher—instead of
choosing whether to become a teacher or a card dealer in
Las Vegas! Sometimes the choices before you seem
equally right on the basis of the principles set forth in the
Word of God.

At such times, the benefit of the Scriptures as a means
of communication cannot be overemphasized—along
with making use of all eight of the steps in knowing God's

will. For God may be able to communicate His specific will to you in some other manner than through chapter and verse.

There may be times when God will surprise you with how specific passages of Scripture apply to your situation, when you have come to Him for guidance on a specific decision. It's happened to me perhaps half a dozen times during my lifetime, when the Word of God suddenly spoke to my present decision in an unmistakable manner.

One summer I sold Christian books to earn the money to return to college in the fall. The first day my sales manager came out to show me how to sell books. While I stood there and held the briefcase, he sold books all day long. It looked easy! I went home elated and multiplied the number of books we had sold that first day by the number of days in the summer, and was sure that I would return in the fall with three or four times the money I needed for school.

Then the sales manager left town. Day after day was the same. I didn't sell a single book. Before long I was very discouraged. Now it didn't look like I'd make even one scholarship. In fact, it was easy to believe that the rest of the summer could go by and I wouldn't make even one sale! One night I was so discouraged I could hardly sleep. The next morning I was trying to decide what to do. Should I go home and forget the whole thing? Should I keep trying, even though it appeared to be hopeless? I was impressed to open the Bible, and the text I turned to was in Psalm 42:11: "Why art thou cast down, O my soul? and why art thou disquieted within me? hope thou in God: for I shall yet praise him, who is the health of my countenance, and my God."

This message from God's Word gave me the courage to try again. On my way out to work, I stopped by the post office. There was a letter waiting for me from a woman to whom I had shown the books three days before. She had decided she was interested! I spun gravel all the way out to her house and made my first sale that morning. The Lord had begun to show me that I didn't sell His books. He did. If you have ever tried to sell Christian books, you've learned that lesson as well.

One time when my wife and I were pastoring a church in Oregon we received a call to another place and were trying to learn God's will for us in that decision. One morning I was down in the basement, in my study, praying about the matter, and felt impressed to open the Bible for guidance. The text that jumped out at me was this: "He that remaineth in this city shall die . . . : but he that goeth forth . . . shall live." Jeremiah 38:2. I'd never even seen the text before, and would have to search to find it today. But I pondered it carefully and wondered if it was meant for our situation at that time. I didn't know who in that city was trying to kill me! But it seemed to be speaking to the decision I had just been praying about.

Before mentioning it to anyone, I went upstairs for breakfast. Our son, then six years old, had his little Rainbow Bible at the breakfast table. I said, "Son, choose a text for us to read this morning before our prayer."

He said, "What shall I pick?"

I said, "It doesn't matter. Pick anything."

He opened his little Bible at random and pointed to a verse, handing the Bible to me so that I could read what he had chosen. I took the Bible and read, "He that remaineth in this city shall die . . . : but he that goeth forth . . . shall live."

Now we didn't make our entire decision based on this Bible text, even though we were impressed, for the odds of such a thing happening by chance were overwhelming.

But we put it in the portfolio and considered it along with the rest of the guidance from the Lord on the other steps for knowing His will. It was part of the weight of evidence that led us to accept the call and move from that place.

Then there was the time in Mountain View, California. We loved the church and the people. We didn't want to leave. We particularly didn't want to move to the smog of southern California, which is where our next call led us. We said No. We did not find ourselves with no will of our own on the given matter! But the Lord began to turn us around, and one morning at worship my wife turned to the verse where God told Phillip to *go toward the south, to the place which is called desert.* See Acts 8:26. After three years in southern California, we were delighted to find another text, after being invited back to northern California, which read, "Ye have compassed this mountain long enough: turn you northward." Deuteronomy 2:3.

Now there is a very real hazard that I have discovered in telling these kinds of stories, because people often forget everything else that has been said. They forget the other steps for knowing God's will and begin trying to find God's will solely on the basis of putting their fingers on texts. There is no safety in using this as the only method for determining God's will.

Often you will discover, if you try to do it yourself, without being led to such a thing by the Holy Spirit, that you will end up in the "begats" somewhere, with nothing that could even look like guidance. I've had it happen on occasion. There is also the story told of the person who tried this as a form of guidance, apart from any other method, and turned to two texts. The first one said, "And Judas went out and hanged himself," and the second said, "Go, and do thou likewise." Matthew 27:5; Luke 10:37. Fairly certain that God didn't mean for him to take his own life, he put his finger on a third text, and it said, "That thou doest, do quickly." John 13:27.

So I would like to go on record as *not* recommending this as the method for discovering God's will. However, as you continue in the relationship with Him and seek to learn His will by all of the methods which He has given, there may come times when He will choose to communicate with you through His Word by leading you to a specific text that expresses His will for you at that time. Perhaps it would be helpful at such times to remember that He will not give specific counsel from a random text that goes against the general counsel of His Word, in terms of principles and truth. You may also find that at such times He speaks to you in the very words you have been presenting to Him, in your prayers on the subject. Even in the day-by-day devotional relationship with God, it is often the case that you will come across something in your reading for that particular day that answers the very question you had in your mind, that you had been wondering about.

Some people may be uneasy with such a subjective method of communication with God, yet for those who question whether or not God would ever use such a plan, it may help to remember that this should never be the entire basis of a decision. But God may at times choose to make it part of the package, working in a mysterious way His wonders to perform.

In Psalm 32:8 we read, "I will instruct thee and teach thee in the way which thou shalt go: I will guide thee with mine eye." If you go to 1 Corinthians 12, you discover that the church is likened to the human body, with different parts having different functions, but all working together for the good of the whole. Just because you are one of the members of the body that seems small and insignificant doesn't mean that your place is unimportant. If any part of the body is hurting, the whole body feels the pain.

Paul makes the comparison between the human body and the various members of the body of Christ. And in that context, there is an interesting text found in 1 Samuel 9:9. "Beforetime in Israel, when a man went to enquire of God, thus he spake, Come, and let us go to the seer: for he that is now called a Prophet was beforetime called a Seer." Have you ever examined that Old Testament word? What is a seer? Well, a see-er is one who does the seeing! Therefore, the prophet of the Old Testament was likened to the eyes of the church.

So when we consult the Bible and the word of the prophet of God, we are given help in knowing the will of the Lord. Could this be one of the ways in which God "guides us with His *eye*"? Don't sell that short as you consult the inspired counsel from the Lord that has been given to the church. We will have many occasions to be thankful for the help and guidance that has been given through the eyes of the church.

How thankful we can be for the gift of God's Word, for His voice through His prophets, to guide and direct us in the way in which He would have us go. It provides a powerful and dependable source for knowing the will of God, when we *consult God's Word*.

Step 4
God's Will and His Providence

Let's begin by doing an exhaustive study of the word *providence* in the Bible—or in the King James Version at least! It's easily done, for there is only one reference, found in Acts 24:2. Notice the first few verses: "After five days Ananias the high priest descended with the elders, and with a certain orator named Tertullus, who informed the governor against Paul. And when he was called forth, Tertullus began to accuse him, saying, Seeing that by thee we enjoy great quietness, and that very worthy deeds are done unto this nation by thy *providence*, we accept it always, and in all places, most noble Felix, with all thankfulness. Notwithstanding, that I be not further tedious unto thee, I pray thee that thou wouldest hear us of thy clemency a few words."

This oily-mouthed orator went on to try to persuade the governor to put a stop to Paul's work in preaching the gospel. But he used the word *providence*. He wasn't speaking of the providence of God, but rather of the providence of the governor. He was talking about what the governor had provided for his subjects. So when we use the word *providence* in reference to God's guidance in our lives, we are speaking of the things God has provided for us.

This fourth step in knowing God's will in our lives is to *consider providential circumstances*. The providence of God may be a little harder to explain, or to understand, than some of the other steps in knowing God's will, so let's use an illustration. Try thinking of your life as a jigsaw puzzle. Each event is a separate piece of the puzzle. As you put together the puzzle, piece by piece, a picture emerges, which reveals the plan for your life.

Have you ever put a puzzle together? It's relatively easy to start out with, when you look for all the edge pieces and link them together. But then it gets harder. If you stay with it through the harder part, it can be actually exciting to get in those last few pieces!

We have a friend who loves to put puzzles together. She prided herself on being a puzzle expert. She could get a puzzle together faster than anyone else around. One year at Christmas my wife found her a puzzle for a gift. It was a picture of Little Red Riding Hood's hood. It was solid red! It took her twenty hours to put together, and we all rejoiced!

Remembering how a puzzle fits together can be one method for recognizing the providence of God, to see His dealings with you in the past and realize where He has led you so far. You might want to actually sit down with a piece of paper and pencil and list all of the major events in the last five or ten years of your life. Do you see a picture emerging? Does the decision you are now trying to make fit into that picture?

Suppose a student comes by my office for advice on how to decide which should be his lifework. As we spend a little time getting acquainted, I ask him about his interests and hobbies so far in his experience.

He says, "My father is a veterinarian. I have always loved animals. As a child, I was always bringing home some animal that was hurt or hungry and nursing it back to health.

"Summers I have worked in the office with my father, and loved it. The time always goes by so fast in the summer. During the school year, my favorite subject has been biology, although I've done well in the other science classes too. And I have a scholarship to a veterinary college. But what I'm trying to decide is whether or not God wants me to be an auto mechanic."

This would be an extreme example of a puzzle piece that didn't fit, when it came to considering providential circumstances.

Of course, we shouldn't decide solely on the basis of the puzzle pieces, any more than we should decide on the basis of any other single step. But it may be that to look carefully at the leading of God in your past experiences will provide insights into the current decision with which you are faced.

There are exceptions to the rule about puzzles. Sometimes God is working on more than one picture in your life at one time, and a new decision may fit into the new picture He wants to make in your life, even when it doesn't seem to fit into the old picture at all.

It happened that way for Moses. He thought he was supposed to lead God's people out of Egypt, but things weren't moving along quickly enough to suit him, so he jumped in and got some action going himself. He got one Egyptian. Then he fled before Pharaoh, out across the desert sands, and for forty years herded his father-in-law's sheep on the back side of the mountain. He didn't even have his own herd of sheep!

Then one day God met him there in the desert at a burning bush and reminded him of the call to be the deliverer of the people of God. And Moses said, "You've got the wrong man. I'm a born sheepherder. Not only that, You've waited too long. I've even forgotten the language. You'll have to send somebody else."

Moses didn't think the puzzle piece fit at all. But God was still at work in his life; and His purposes, which know no haste and no delay, were ready for fulfillment.

David was also a shepherd. As he herded his father's flocks he heard from his brothers about wars and fighting. They were soldiers in the king's army. Even Samuel, when God sent him to anoint David to be king of Israel, had trouble passing up David's brothers, who seemed to be far more qualified for the job.

But God had a new picture to make in David's life, and He warned Samuel not to look at outward appearances. See 1 Samuel 16:7. The call to be king didn't seem to fit. In fact, as David fled from Saul for seven years, it didn't seem like it was ever going to be realized! David, Moses, and many other godly people had to wait for years before the completion of God's plan in their lives. But the plan of God was fulfilled in the end.

This brings us to another important point to remember when considering providential circumstances: God moves on a different timetable than we do. He seems to delight in waiting until the last minute! He didn't open the Red Sea for the people of Israel when they first arrived at its banks. He waited until the Egyptian armies had caught up with them and were ready to close in for the kill. He didn't sweeten the waters of Marah until after the people of Israel had tested them and found that they were bitter. He didn't intervene with fire from heaven until the last minute of the last day of the final showdown between God and Baal.

You may discover in your own life that God has the same habit today. If it looks like you are in financial trouble and that in thirty days you will be faced with bank-ruptcy, relax! You've got twenty-nine days—or maybe even twenty-nine and a half days, before God needs to move in your behalf.

In our human impatience, we often think God could hurry up a little! But God has more on His agenda than simply bringing deliverance for each particular crisis. He also wants to teach us important lessons of trust and dependence upon Him. He wants to give us insights into our own hearts and what makes us tick.

What happens inside of you when God waits? Are you able to move ahead calmly, trusting Him to bring deliverance in His own time and way? Or are you tempted, as Moses was, to take matters into your own hands? Do you become angry with God for not moving at your speed? And could it be good for you to see how easily you become angry with God, how quickly you stop trusting Him and begin to trust in your own feeble strength?

As you learn the lesson of waiting, even when it seems like disaster and defeat are close at hand, you will come to appreciate the providence of God which doesn't always come immediately. It becomes an exciting thing to wait and watch for Him to work His miracles in your life.

Another way in which God's providence works is through divine appointments, through crossing your path with people who have information you may need to make the right decision.

Perhaps you are trying to decide what kind of car to buy. You've been to the car dealer and heard his sales pitch. You've done some checking on your own as to the merits of the particular brand and model you're interested in buying.

But you've been through this kind of decision before and gotten some real lemons. So you begin to invite the

Lord to guide you in this decision, and to your amazement, within a short time, you see His providence at work. You run into other people, seemingly by accident, who have had experience with the very kind of car you're thinking of getting. They didn't know about the decision you were trying to make, but somehow the conversation took a turn in that direction, and you profit from their experience. Have you ever had that sort of thing happen?

Not long ago we received an invitation to hold some meetings in Florida for a particular group. They invited us to bring along the whole family, since the meetings were being held over the Christmas holidays. After discussing it, our family decided to accept the offer.

But we have some young people in our family who would not want to spend all of their Christmas vacation sitting in meetings. And that's OK, isn't it? So we were wondering what sort of activities we could include that would make the vacation as enjoyable for them as possible.

We remembered an offer that had been made several years back by some friends who had a summer cottage not far from where the meetings were to be held. So far we had never had occasion to accept their offer, but now we thought of it and tried to get in touch with them. Unfortunately, we had lost their address, and we couldn't find anyone who could tell us where they were.

My wife, without even telling the rest of the family about it until afterward, began to pray that God would provide a place for us to stay for the week of meetings. A few days later we met some people for the first time and had lunch with them. Over lunch, they told us they had a beach house in Florida and that we could use it if we ever needed such a thing!

The beach house which the Lord provided was superior

to the original vacation cottage that we had in mind, for it was right on the beach, and our young people could make use of the sun and sand whenever they wanted to.

We had made the decision to attend the meetings even before receiving the offer of the beach house! But as we considered all of the ways of recognizing God's leading in our lives, His providence in the matter of the beach house became one of the reasons why we felt sure God was leading us to that particular place at that time.

Jesus accepted the Father's guidance in making divine appointments when He was here on earth. He was willing to walk fifty miles out of His way just to place Himself in the path of one Syrophoenician woman who was longing for His presence and help. He was willing to forget about resting and eating and even getting a drink of water to cool Him in the hot afternoon sun, in order to minister to the woman of Samaria as He sat by the well. He was willing to put off going to bed at the end of a busy day in order to visit with Nicodemus, who was ashamed to come during regular "office hours"! He allowed His Father to make the plans and then to reveal them to Him on a daily basis, during His time of communion with His Father.

Have you seen the Lord at work in your life, in bringing you divine appointments? It's another facet of His providential leading at work. Maybe you are looking for some opportunity to witness for the gospel. You begin to pray about it, and before long He crosses your path with people who are in need of the very kind of help you have to offer. In fact, on the basis of my own experience, as well as the case histories that others have shared with me, I am willing to predict that God will bring you an average of one a day of this kind of opportunity if you are sensitive to His guidance and invite Him to do so.

You may find that the divine appointments interrupt

your own plans, but if you are willing to be interrupted, God's providence will lead you in exciting ways.

The timing of divine appointments is always right. Sometimes you may be faced with what looks like a divine appointment, but the timing is wrong. You can know that it is not the hand of the Lord that is working.

When we accepted the call to leave beautiful northern California and go to Nebraska, we prayed and considered and went through the various steps for learning God's will. Then we made a decision. The time for our final answer arrived, and we couldn't put it off any longer. Based on all of the information we had gained, based on all that was in the portfolio from each of the eight steps, we decided that the Lord was leading us to accept the call to Nebraska. We officially accepted the offer.

The following week, I got a call from a close friend who is a radio evangelist. His daughter lived in the town we were leaving and had told him about our decision to move to Nebraska.

He said, "Hello, Brother Venden. This is your conscience speaking!" And he proceeded to tell me all the reasons he could think of why we should stay in northern California. He had some pretty impressive reasons, and he was someone whose counsel I had prized and whose wisdom I had respected. If he had made that call a week earlier, that one thing might have swayed the decision the other way, in spite of the evidence from the other steps in knowing the Lord's will! But the timing was wrong. The decision had already been made, doors were opening in that direction, and I could not listen to his voice, even though, humanly speaking, it was extremely difficult to go against his counsel.

As we seek for the guidance of the Holy Spirit in the decisions of our lives, we can see His hand at work in divine appointments, either causing or preventing contacts that will influence our choices. Have you ever had it happen in your life? You try and try to get in touch with some person, and every time you call, the line is busy or they just left or they should have been back by now but they're not, and nothing you do can bring you together. Or have you ever found the reverse to be true? You run into the same person fifteen times in a single day, until you are finally willing to speak to them or listen to them and recognize a divine appointment. God's ways of working are often mysterious to our human understanding, but the path of His providence brings us divine appointments as one of the common methods He chooses for the revealing of His will.

There is another area of providence, a darker side, that we would often escape if we had the choice. God's providence often leads us through the trials and troubles that we face in this world of sin. He doesn't bring the trouble, but His providence can guide us through it. Any barrier that the hosts of darkness can throw in our pathway, God can turn into a steppingstone to the fulfillment of His plan in our lives.

Remember Joseph? As he rode off into the night, his father's tents disappearing on the far horizon, it looked like the end of everything. How could such betrayal by his brothers and ill treatment by the slave traders be part of God's plan for his life? Things looked a little more promising for a while there in Egypt, as he became more and more trusted and relied upon in the house of Potiphar. But his time of favor was short-lived, and as he spent day after day and night after night imprisoned in the Egyptian dungeon, his faith and trust in God were sorely tested. It was the dark side of the providence of God that allowed him to be brought to such a place. But it was nonetheless the providence of God, for the trials which He permitted to come to Joseph were the very things which prepared Joseph for his work as a deliverer, not only of Egypt, not only of his own family, but of the surrounding nations as well.

David fleeing from an angry and jealous Saul, Jeremiah in the mud pit, John the Baptist in Herod's dungeon, John the Beloved on the Isle of Patmos—the list could go on and on. Times without number, the providence of God has led His people through the dark and lonely pathways. In our human weakness, we rejoice far more when Daniel is delivered from the lions than when John the Baptist was beheaded. But the loving providence is leading in each case. The promise is still sure that "all things work together for good to them that love God, to them who are the called according to his purpose." Romans 8:28.

We find it hard to understand that it is no greater evidence of the favor and guidance of God to be whisked off to heaven in a chariot of fire than to die of a long, lingering illness. Elisha was just as honored of God as was Elijah, and both were guided by His providence in fulfilling their part in His divine purpose. Fellowship with Christ in His suffering, as well as fellowship with Him in service and fellowship with Him in His glory, are promised to His faithful followers. And even when His choice for us seems far removed from what we would choose for ourselves, we can still trust Him with our lives. As the song says:

> The path that I have trod, has brought me nearer God,
> Though oft it led through sorrow's gate.
> Though not the way I'd choose, in my way I might lose
> The joys that yet for me await.

The area of providential circumstances can be one of the most exciting of the eight steps, for it is one that is completely in God's department. He's the One who chooses the time and the method for communicating to you through His providences. Providential circumstances are not something that can be easily duplicated by human power. And even when we do not understand the reasons for His providential working, it provides one of the most unmistakable evidences of His leading to the one who is seeking to know His will.

As you try to be sensitive to God's will in your life, learning what it means by His grace to have no will of your own, and daily seeking to know Him through His Word and through prayer and communion with Him, the leading of His providence becomes very meaningful. His leading in your past, as well as the providences He brings into your present, can give real insight into His will as you *consider providential circumstances.*

Step 5
God's Will and Your Friends

Several years ago up in Oregon a young bachelor preacher moved to his first parish. In the church were two unmarried older women who were sisters. They became very interested in the new preacher.

Before long, their mother arranged to have the new preacher over for dinner after church. And after dinner, one of the women cornered him in the living room, and she was all excited. She had good news for him. She said, "The Lord has revealed to me that we are to be married!"

His answer was a classic. He replied, "That's interesting. Now when the Lord reveals the same thing to me, we'll be married!"

A woman came to see me in Los Angeles one time and said, "Pastor, the Lord has revealed to me that there is gold up in Alaska. He has showed me the exact spot where it will be found. All we have to do is take along a broom, sweep away the snow, pick it up, and bring it back. And you are supposed to go with me."

I remembered the bachelor preacher from Oregon and said, "That's interesting. When the Lord reveals the same thing to me, I'll go with you."

She said, "You will? Really?"

"Yes, when the Lord reveals the same thing to me."

She went away excited and satisfied with my answer! I had a suspicion that she was having problems with her "filaments"—and time proved that to be the case. We didn't go with our brooms to Alaska.

But while we cannot *depend* on others to be the channel for the Lord to reveal His will to us, the counsel of others is an important step in understanding the will of the Lord. So step five in knowing God's will in your life is to *counsel with godly friends*.

This is the one step that I have added to Mueller's original list of seven steps. It's found in a number of places in Scripture. Psalm 1:1 says, "Blessed is the man that walketh not in the counsel of the ungodly." Notice that the warning is against counseling with the ungodly—not the godly. So when Proverbs 11:14 tells us, "Where no counsel is, the people fall: but in the multitude of counsellors there is safety," it must be talking about the counsel of the godly, not the ungodly.

There are good counselors and there are bad counselors. This is one of the problems in the counseling world in general. As you know, counseling has become popular in recent years, and there is a great deal of counseling going on. But just counsel is not enough. It is important to receive godly counsel if you are interested in learning more about God's will in your life. It is possible to misunderstand what makes a counselor a godly counselor. Just because a person belongs to the Christian church does not make him a Christian counselor.

So when we include counsel with Christian friends as one of the eight steps in learning God's will in our lives, we should seek counsel from godly people, not from the ungodly.

What is a godly person? What is it that makes a person a Christian? The Bible says the Lord knows how to deliver the godly out of temptation. That's an interesting way to say it. Evidently the Lord does not know how to deliver the ungodly out of temptation. What does it mean to be godly? A person who is godly would be one who is very much involved with God.

Often we measure Christianity and godliness by behavior, when we should measure it by relationship. That's the constant key in the whole realm of righteousness by faith. Relationship. And regardless of whether a person claims to be a Christian counselor or not, the only Christian counselor is the one who has a personal relationship with the Lord Jesus Christ.

There have been many who have hung out their shingles and claimed to be Christian counselors who are not that at all. And the symptoms are easy to find. The person who is a Christian counselor is one who will direct you to dependence upon Jesus. It is the non-Christian counseling world at large that invites you to depend upon yourself or to depend upon them instead.

In the secular world, the one who is considered a good counselor will allow you to depend on him just long enough to get you to depend upon yourself again. A bad secular counselor will try to keep you dependent upon him in order to make more money. But a Christian counselor will help you to place your trust in the Lord Jesus as your only help, your only hope.

There are a number of Bible examples of people who asked counsel of others in trying to understand the will of the Lord. Let's look first at a few examples of the ones who sought counsel from the wrong sources.

First Kings 12 tells about Rehoboam, the son of Solomon. Solomon was gone, and Rehoboam had succeeded him on the throne. As he began to take over the government of the kingdom, a delegation of people came to him with a request. They said, "Thy father made our yoke grievous: now therefore make thou the grievous service of thy father, and his heavy yoke which he put upon us, lighter, and we will serve thee." 1 Kings 12:4.

In departing from the Lord in the later years of his life, Solomon had levied heavy taxes upon the people in order to build up his kingdom to an even greater level of luxury and extravagance. The people were tired of the heavy taxes and hoped for a change with the new government.

Rehoboam replied, "Depart yet for three days, then come again to me. And the people departed." Verse 5.

Do you remember the story? Rehoboam called in the old counselors. They advised that he go along with the request of the delegation and make the load lighter, thus gaining the loyalty and support of the people. But Rehoboam didn't stop there. He turned to the younger men, who were ambitious and greedy and immature, as he himself apparently was. The young counselors said, "Make the yoke heavier." They said, "Thus shalt thou speak unto this people that spake unto thee, saying, Thy father made our yoke heavy, but make thou it lighter unto us; thus shalt thou say unto them, My little finger shall be thicker than my father's loins. And now whereas my father did lade you with a heavy yoke, I will add to your yoke: my father hath chastised you with whips, but I will chastise you with scorpions." Verses 10, 11.

Rehoboam listened to the counsel of the younger men. That was part of his problem. But perhaps the greater problem was that there is no evidence that he consulted the Lord in the matter. He went by his own judgment and chose to follow the advice of the younger men. As a result the kingdom was divided, and Israel and Judah were at each other's throats for years following his poor decision. Ten of the twelve tribes pulled away from his heavier yoke, and he was left with only a fraction of the people under his authority. He listened to the wrong counsel.

Maybe this tells us something. We have to be old enough to die before we know enough to live. We are too soon old, and too late smart. Any fool can learn by his own mistakes. It takes a wise person to learn by the experience of others. Rehoboam didn't listen to the men of experience, and terrible were the results of his poor judgment.

Let's look at another interesting Old Testament story, found in 1 Kings 22. The kingdom has been divided now, and there are two sections—Israel and Judah. Ahab was king of one, and Jehoshaphat was king of the other. Ahab went to his rival king, Jehoshaphat, and asked him to join with him in fighting a common enemy—Ramoth-gilead.

In verse 5, "Jehoshaphat said unto the king of Israel, Enquire, I pray thee, at the word of the Lord to day."

So Ahab gathered his prophets together, about 400 of them, and asked, "Shall I go against Ramoth-gilead to battle, or shall I forbear? And they said, Go up; for the Lord shall deliver it into the hand of the king." Verse 6.

But Jehoshaphat wasn't satisfied. He said in verse 7, "Is there not here a prophet of the Lord besides, that we might enquire of him?" Jehoshaphat was a godly man, as you may recall. Ahab was not. He married the wrong woman and followed her into all sorts of wickedness. But apparently Ahab desperately needed the help of Jehoshaphat in this particular battle, for he was willing to go along with Jehoshaphat's request. He said, "There is yet one man, Micaiah the son of Imlah, by whom we may inquire of the Lord: but I hate him; for he doth not prophesy good concerning me, but evil." Verse 8.

And Jehoshaphat said, "Let not the king say so." In other words, "Don't say that! You're just being paranoid!"

So the king commanded that Micaiah be called in before him.

The messenger who went to call Micaiah tried to help things along as best he could. He told him, "Behold now, the words of the prophets declare good unto the king with one mouth: let thy word, I pray thee, be like the word of one of them, and speak that which is good." Verse 13.

Micaiah replied, "As the Lord liveth, what the Lord saith unto me, that will I speak." Verse 14. But if that was the case, the Lord gave him interesting words to say, because when he came before King Ahab and was asked the question, "Shall we go against Ramoth-gilead to battle, or shall we forbear?" He answered by saying, "Go, and prosper: for the Lord shall deliver it into the hand of the king." Verse 15.

Somehow, Ahab realized that Micaiah wasn't leveling with him. Perhaps he had a twinkle in his eye. But his reply is almost funny, for he said, "How many times shall I adjure thee that thou tell me nothing but that which is true in the name of the Lord?" Verse 16.

Then Micaiah gave the Lord's message. He said, "I saw all Israel scattered upon the hills, as sheep that have not a shepherd: and the Lord said, These have no master: let them return every man to his house in peace." Verse 17.

But instead of appreciating the warning sent of God, Ahab said peevishly to Jehoshaphat, "Did I not tell thee that he would prophesy no good concerning me, but evil?" Verse 18.

Ahab recognized the voice of the Lord in the second message of Micaiah, but he was unwilling to accept it. He went into battle against Ramoth-gilead, and that was the end of Ahab. It was during the battle that he was killed.

It is a solemn truth to realize that we not only must learn what God's will is in our lives, but we must also receive from Him power to follow His will, or we will find ourselves in the shoes of Ahab.

Back in 1957 I needed a car. A Christian used-car dealer showed me a '53 Cadillac that had been driven by a little old school teacher from Pasadena. It looked good to me! I had always wanted a Cadillac, with the wall-to-wall carpets, the quiet engine, and the smooth ride. It took a bit of talking to convince my wife, but I told her all about how it would never wear out, never depreciate, get terrific gas mileage, and was half the price of a new Chevy! My mind was made up from the time I first test drove that Cadillac, and nothing anyone said on the negative side even registered. I was like Rehoboam, and like Ahab. Even if I suspected that my decision to buy that car was a wrong decision, I wanted it so badly that I had no power to keep from getting it!

So finally I had my Cadillac. My church members began ribbing me about my Cadillac, and before long, when I'd go to visit somebody, I'd drive my car down two blocks and over three blocks to park, and then walk back five, so they wouldn't see my car!

But the radiator was rusted out, and soon the car overheated and cracked the engine. Of course, the cylinders filled up with water, and it wouldn't start. So I got my neighbor to push me, and that made the transmission go out.

Not long after that, the rear end went out. Then I discovered that the wall-to-wall carpeting was all moldy and rotten underneath. By the time I had replaced the radiator and the transmission and the rear end and the carpeting, I wasn't as fond of Cadillacs as I had been before!

We have all probably had times in our lives when we listened to the wrong counsel and had to live with the consequences of our poor choices. But there are also encouraging examples in Scripture of those who listened to the godly counsel that was offered to them and thus saved themselves from many defeats.

Moses was one. His father-in-law came for a visit, out there in the desert sands, and watched as Moses was called from one dispute to another all day long, from early morning till late at night. He became concerned. He realized that Moses' strength was not equal to the task of handling all those people single-handedly, so he offered some wise counsel. He suggested that Moses reorganize things. Moses recognized his counsel as from the Lord. You can read about it in Exodus 18. Jethro suggested that Moses find able men who feared God, whom he could appoint to be rulers over the people: rulers of thousands, and of hundreds, and of fifties, and of tens. He recommended that they be given the authority to handle all the small problems that might arise, bringing only the more difficult matters to the attention of Moses himself.

Jethro said, "If thou shalt do this thing, and God command thee so, then thou shalt be able to endure, and all this people shall also go to their place in peace. So Moses hearkened to the voice of his father in law, and did all that he said." Exodus 18:23, 24.

One of the first places to look for godly counsel is right in your own family! It would be an unfortunate family indeed who would have such a fanatical family member as to believe that God only guides him, by himself, and not the family as a unit.

My wife and I were very happy pastoring in Mountain View, California, several years ago. When the invitation came to move to southern California, our entire family was negative about going. But the people at the new church kept asking and said they'd pay for our trip down just to look, so finally we agreed to go for a visit. We said,

"We'll enjoy a trip to visit—but we're not coming!"

So my wife and my son and I went to southern California. We went into the office of the administrator who had invited us, and my wife and son slumped down into their chairs and stared out the window. I was embarrassed! After we left, I said, "Look, you don't have to act like that. You can at least be civil. We've already told them we're not coming."

We went to the church and attended a reception in our honor but it was hard work. All of us were relieved when we left. We drove home, across the Mojave Desert, toward beautiful northern California.

As we drove along, I said to my wife and son, "Well, now you can relax. We're not moving." And in my heart I said to the Lord, "The only way I could move to southern California would be if there was a drastic change of attitude on the part of my wife and my boy." And I relaxed too!

We got home, parked the car in the garage, unpacked our things, and I thought the matter was closed. But the next morning my boy met me first thing. He said, "Dad?"

"Yes?"

"I think we're supposed to move to southern California.

Later that same day, without any communication with our son, my wife came to the same conclusion. We began to reconsider and realized that we very well may have missed it on step one—having no will of our own in the matter.

A couple of days later, in family worship, we turned to the story I mentioned previously where God instructed someone to "*go toward the south, to the place that is called desert.*" It was from Acts 8, the story of the Ethiopian and Phillip. And as the evidence accumulated from the eight steps for knowing God's will, the time came when we agreed, all of us together, to accept the call to southern California.

So God may lead through your family. He may also lead through the members of the body of Christ. It happened that way in Acts 4, when Peter and John had been arrested and beaten for preaching the gospel of Jesus Christ. They were warned by the authorities not to speak in His name anymore. The first thing they did was to return to their own company and tell them what had happened. This group went to their knees immediately and lifted up their voices to God. As a result, the early apostles were filled with such zeal through the power of the Holy Spirit that they had the courage and boldness to continue to speak and share the good news of Jesus.

Remember, though, that whether you are considering the counsel of your family, your close friends, or the members of your church, you should not make your entire decision on the basis of their counsel. We continue to warn on this point: do not decide on the basis of *any* single step. Rather, put them all together, and make your decision from the weight of evidence.

When Jesus was here on earth, at the beginning of His ministry, His mother called Him to her at the wedding feast at Cana and told Him of a problem with the wine. While Jesus saw fit to answer her request, His words gently reminded her that He had to stand free to do the will of His Father in heaven. Not even His mother was given the job of directing His mission, apart from the will of His heavenly Father. He had responded in the same way when He was only twelve years old, when He was left behind in the temple. And at the close of His life, when His mother and brothers wanted Him to modify His manner of teaching and ministering in order to fit their ideas, He refused. He was kind, respectful, and loving, but He did not allow His family to have complete control over His decision.

At the same time, for the majority of His life here on earth He was subject to His parents, working in the carpenter shop, involved in the life of the family that had been given Him by His Father.

The members of your family, or your close friends, even godly friends, or the members of your church, may be an avenue through which God can speak to you, though they may not always be used in that way. Even if your family and friends and fellow church members are sincere followers of God themselves and are in touch with Him, God may choose to close their eyes temporarily to the messages He is sending you in order that you may learn to hear His voice for yourself and not depend upon other people to do your thinking and praying and studying for you. In the end, the greatest counsel of all comes from the One who is called the wonderful Counselor, the mighty God, the everlasting Father, the Prince of Peace. He is recommended to us, in our search to know His will. Are you in touch with Him? Do you know what it means to hear His voice for yourself, to recognize His guidance in your life?

He is in the business of guiding His people, and what a blessing He brings through those who love us, and who love Him, when we *counsel with Christian friends.*

Step 6
God's Will
and Your Prayer

We have taken the position that step one, to have no
will of your own in the given matter, is the most difficult
of all the steps. And many have found that step eight, the
last step in knowing God's will in your life, is the most
exciting, because there's where you begin to see the foot-
prints of heavenly forces at work in a very direct way. But
step six is the most important of all of the steps, to *Ask
God to guide you in the decision you are going to make.*

If there were time for only one of the eight steps, this
would be the one that should be chosen above all others—
prayer. There is nothing more vital to the life of the
Christian, and there is nothing more indispensable when
it comes to learning the will of God.

Prayer has often been neglected and underrated. Often
we proceed with our own planning and devising, and after
we have already made up our minds what we are going to
do, how we are going to proceed, we suddenly remember
to say a token prayer. Have you ever been present at a
committee meeting, and after perhaps several hours of
discussing the pros and cons, and finally bringing matters to a vote, just before everyone is ready to go home and
call it a day, someone says, "Shouldn't we have a word of
prayer before we close?"

In listing prayer as step six, we are in nowise trying to place a priority on the steps for knowing God's will in your life. Prayer is needed in combination with every one of the steps. Without prayer, we have no hope of coming to the place of having no will of our own. Without prayer, the reading of God's Word can prove a positive injury rather than a blessing. Perhaps the greatest benefit we can gain from counseling with our Christian friends is to enlist their prayers for us, and with us, in the decisions we face. Prayer is vital from the beginning to the end of the process of seeking the guidance of the Lord, because prayer is vital from the beginning to the end of the Christian life.

When Nehemiah was sorrowing over the lack of progress that was being made in the rebuilding of the temple, the king noticed his sad countenance and inquired concerning its cause. Nehemiah was surprised. He wasn't planning to discuss his problems and the problems of his people with the king. Then the king surprised Nehemiah even further by saying, "For what dost thou make request?" Nehemiah 2:4.

Nehemiah didn't have time to carefully consider providential circumstances or consult with his godly friends. He had time for just one thing—the most important thing—and immediately, right there in the presence of the king, he made use of this most important step in learning the will of God. It says, "So I prayed to the God of heaven."

In that same instant, before trying to answer the king in his own wisdom, Nehemiah sought for the guidance of the Lord, and it was given to him. The words to speak, the right request to make, was given to him on the spot.

You may often find yourself in positions where an immediate decision is required. Perhaps on the highway, a split-second choice is forced upon you. You can try to operate in your own wisdom, or you can do as Peter did in his emergency on the sea, and cry, "Lord, save me." Perhaps in trying to help a friend or neighbor or family member you find yourself not knowing what words to say. You have the choice of relying on your own wisdom or sending a silent prayer to heaven for assistance and wisdom from above. You may need to make a choice in connection with business matters that you had not anticipated and for which you have not had time to spend in pursuing the eight steps. You can trust your own judgment, or you can call upon the name of the Lord as Nehemiah did, and place the burden of the decision upon Him.

But here again we are reminded of the importance, of the absolute necessity of spending time in communion and prayer with God day by day, *before* a crisis hits. Through our fellowship and relationship with Him day by day, God can become so near to us that whenever we are faced with an unexpected trial or decision, our thoughts will spontaneously turn to Him as naturally as the flower turns to the sun. The reverse is also true. If we neglect to commune with God on a regular basis, when the crisis comes, He will be far from our thoughts, and we will naturally and spontaneously try to save ourselves and rely upon our own feeble wisdom and strength.

However, in the area of prayer, there are many insights and understandings that can be gained that will make this most important step more meaningful and understandable, and for this reason we are going to consider the place and function of prayer in seeking to know the will of God in our lives.

The first principle in this connection would be to underline its importance, as we have been attempting to do in the preceding paragraphs. We are invited to ask. We are instructed to ask. Luke 11:9-13 is an example: "Ask, and it shall be given you; seek, and ye shall find; knock, and it shall be opened unto you. For every one that asketh receiveth; and he that seeketh findeth; and to him that knocketh it shall be opened. If a son shall ask bread of any of you that is a father, will he give him a stone? or if he ask a fish, will he for a fish give him a serpent? Or if he shall ask an egg, will he offer him a scorpion? If ye then, being evil, know how to give good gifts unto your children: how much more shall your heavenly Father give the Holy Spirit to them that ask him?" So the Holy Spirit, the faithful Guide, is given in answer to prayer.

Please notice that when we speak of asking God to guide us, we're not recommending asking for a sign. We're not asking Him to send a thunderbolt out of the blue or bring fire down from heaven. All we're doing is taking the matter before Him, specifically, and inviting Him to take control in the way He sees fit.

God does have a will concerning your life. Sometimes people say, "Why, there can be any number of 'right' choices in a given decision. God gave us our brains to figure things out for ourselves, and whatever we decide must be the will of God if we use what common sense and judgment we have been given." But as we noticed earlier, if that were the case, an atheist or infidel could be just as guided by God as the praying Christian.

Jonah reasoned that way when the Lord sent him to Nineveh. He decided, on the basis of his own judgment and common sense, that Tarshish would be just as acceptable a destination. After a few days of seclusion, in a rather interesting location for a "retreat," he seriously reconsidered his position! The Lord has reasons for directing our feet to the places where He chooses to send us. He knew what He was doing when He sent Philip to the Ethiopian, instead of sending Peter or John. He had a specific purpose in bringing the little Israelite maiden to the household of Namaan. He chose Ananias to reach out to the apostle Paul, still blinded by the Damascus light, praying for guidance from above.

While there may be a number of apparently "good" decisions, God alone is in a position to judge if there is a "best" decision and to reveal that to you as you seek to learn His will.

We are not only invited to ask God for guidance in the great decisions of life, but in the small ones as well. In fact, we are given the blessed opportunity of seeking Him in prayer regarding *all* decisions, great or small, and learning His will for us. Philippians 4:6, 7 says, "Be careful for nothing; but in every thing by prayer and supplication with thanksgiving let your requests be made known unto God. And the peace of God, which passeth all understanding, shall keep your hearts and minds through Christ Jesus."

We need to trust far less in what we can do and far more in what God can do for us. The life of the Christian is not departmentalized, with some things small enough to be handled independently and other things important enough to need divine help. There is nothing too small, and nothing too great to bring to God in prayer, allowing Him to control and guide. He is the God for whom nothing is impossible, who upholds the universe with all its worlds and stars and systems. He is also the God who cares for the grass of the field and the sparrow that falls to the ground. He keeps track of the number of hairs on your head. How much more is He interested in being involved in what goes on inside your head!

So although the eight steps for learning God's will can be extremely helpful when it comes to the larger decisions, the one thing that you can always turn to even in the smallest decisions of your life is prayer.

We are invited to ask help for today, and leave tomorrow in God's hands. He does not intend to show us all of the details of our lives at once, or we would be overwhelmed. His plan is to lead His children day by day. In the Sermon on the Mount Jesus said, "Take . . . no thought for the morrow." One of the newer translations of this verse says, "One day's trouble is enough for one day." Matthew 6:34, Phillips.

While it is true that some decisions must be made in advance, the help of God is still offered when it is needed. If you have thirty days before you must give an answer as to whether or not you will move to a new job next July, then you don't necessarily need to know what to decide today. You may begin to pray, but the answer may not come for another twenty-nine days! How much of the confusion and frustration in our lives comes in trying to get ahead of ourselves and live in the future, instead of bringing to God day by day the decisions that need to be made at the present time!

God wants us to bring the details of our lives to share with Him. It makes no difference whether you are making a big decision or a small one, prayer provides an opportunity to share the details with God and seek communion with Him by talking to Him as to a friend.

When we inform our friends of a decision with which we are faced, we go into detail. Whether it's about some major job change or a move to a new part of the country, whether it's about buying one kind of easy chair for the living room or another, we talk through the details. We discuss the pros and cons as we see them. We explain why we lean more toward one choice than another.

It is our privilege as friends of God to discuss things

with Him in just this kind of detail. Hezekiah did it. You've heard of good King Hezekiah. In Isaiah 37:14 it is recorded that he received a threatening, blasphemous letter from Sennacherib. "Hezekiah received the letter from the hand of the messengers, and read it: and Hezekiah went up unto the house of the Lord, and spread it before the Lord."

Didn't God already know what was in the letter? Of course He did. But Hezekiah hadn't yet discussed it with him, so he made a special trip to the temple to do so.

There follows one of the classic prayers of the Bible. Hezekiah presented his arguments as to why God should respond and deliver His people. He started where so many of the great prayers of the Bible started, with a statement of the greatness and power of God. He went on to describe the great need of God's people for deliverance, and he ended his prayer by asking for deliverance from the enemy for God's sake, that His name and reputation might be uplifted before the surrounding nations. The Lord heard, as you recall, and brought about a mighty deliverance for His people.

How long has it been since you spread your case before the Lord when you were faced with some decision? By taking the time to share the details of our lives with God, we give Him an open channel to communicate His will to us.

As we ask God to guide us in the decisions with which we are faced, it is important to learn to watch for His response. Do you expect your prayer for guidance to be answered? Then watch to see in what form the answer comes. The Bible gives all kinds of examples of the methods by which God has responded to His people in their prayers for His guidance and help. God may not always respond in the way you expect. He uses a variety of methods. But watch for His response, because the promise is sure that when you seek Him, you will find Him; when you call upon Him, you will find that He is near.

Remember Nathaniel under the tree, praying for a revelation of God's will in connection with whether or not Jesus was the Messiah? In answer to Nathaniel's prayer, God sent His guidance through a human instrument. Philip came and found him there under the tree, and Nathaniel was able to recognize divine guidance.

The Ethiopian was in his chariot, going home across the desert from Jerusalem. He was asking for wisdom and understanding concerning the things he was reading, and God sent Philip, through miraculous methods, to become the first recorded hitchhiker!

Jehoshaphat was in trouble because the Ammonites and Moabites and all the rest of the "ites" were coming against him to battle, as recorded in 2 Chronicles 20. He called for a prayer meeting, seeking guidance and deliverance from God, and God sent the Spirit of prophecy. A man with a strange name jumped up right in the prayer meeting and gave God's answer to their request.

Balaam, who asked for God's guidance but didn't really want it, was given guidance from a donkey, of all things. Balaam would have done well to listen to his donkey.

Daniel and his companions were threatened with death, along with the so-called wise men of their day, because no one could interpret the king's dream. But in answer to the prayer of Daniel and his friends, seeking guidance from the Lord, Daniel was given the same dream in the night. You know the rest of the story.

On the way from Egypt to Canaan Israel cried out to the Lord for His guidance and protection. For forty years they were guided by the pillar of cloud by day and the pillar of fire by night, a guidance that stayed with them in spite of their sins and failings, their falling and complaining.

Joseph was perplexed by the news that Mary was about to have a baby. He prayed for wisdom to know how to respond to the situation, and God sent an angel in answer to his prayer. The angel said, "Fear not, to take unto thee Mary thy wife." Matthew 1:20.

Joshua, the great general of the armies of Israel, was by Jericho, seeking help from above, and the Captain of the Lord's hosts responded to his prayer for guidance.

When Elijah prayed, after fleeing across the desert for forty days and nights, God responded with a still, small voice, instead of the thunder and fire and wind that Elijah had expected.

There are so many different ways in which God has responded to the prayers of His people. But the tremendous truth of the Bible is that when His children cry out for His help, He responds. And that is still true for the children of God today.

Probably the greatest reason for unanswered prayer today is that we don't pray in the first place! James said it in James 4:2: "Ye have not, because ye ask not."

Are you interested in learning God's will for your life and in receiving power from above to follow His will when it is revealed? The answer is prayer. Much prayer. Constant prayer. Earnest prayer. Persistent prayer. There is no greater method for learning the will of God concerning you than to *ask God to guide you in the decision you are needing to make.*

Step 7
God's Will
and Your Decision

The Bible is filled with calls for decision. After breaking the tables of stone on the rocks of the mountainside and dealing with the problem of the golden calf, Moses called upon the people to decide. He said, "Who is on the Lord's side? let him come unto me." Exodus 32:26. The people were then faced with the consequences of their decision.

Joshua urged the people to decision on the banks of the Jordan River. He said, "Choose you this day whom ye will serve." Joshua 24:15. Elijah, on the top of Mount Carmel, said to the watching multitude, "How long halt ye between two opinions? if the Lord be God, follow him: but if Baal, then follow him." 1 Kings 18:21.

And so in our seeking to know the will of God in our lives, the time comes to *make a decision*. We are not expected to hang by our thumbs forever. We are not to wait for some thunderbolt or supernatural manifestation. After giving a reasonable period of time to consider the various steps in knowing God's will, we arrive at step seven and simply decide. We look at the information we have accumulated so far and make the best decision we can with the information that is available. If it is necessary to err on one side or the other, there is less danger in moving too hastily at times than in spending too long mulling over a decision. The final step in this series of eight steps has a built-in safeguard in case you make a wrong decision.

King Saul had trouble making decisions. He waffled back and forth, one day determining to follow God, the next day choosing his own way instead. One day he honored David and gave him a place near his throne. The next day he tried to pin him to the wall with his javelin. He chased David all over the countryside, trying to kill him. Then David's compassion in not taking Saul's life when the chance presented itself caused Saul to recognize God's hand in David's life and to acknowledge it. He apologized to David for his past behavior. Yet the next thing you know, Saul was out pursuing David once again!

On the other hand, the Bible tells of people such as Daniel, who made a decision for the right and never wavered from that decision, regardless of what the consequences might be.

What made the difference? Why are some people able to arrive at a decision and move ahead with confidence, while others are so indecisive they can't seem to make up their minds whether to get up in the morning? Surely the makeup of the personality has something to do with it, but are we to be victims of our heritage, with no choice in the matter of whether we have the backbone to make a choice and stick with it?

For a Bible answer to this dilemma, let's go to a verse that may not be the first one you'd expect to study in terms of decision making, but which is nevertheless very much to the point. Paul is writing to the believers, and he says," Wherefore, my beloved, as ye have always obeyed, not as in my presence only, but now much more in my absence, work out your own salvation with fear and trembling. For it is God which worketh in you both to will and to do of his good pleasure." Philippians 2:12, 13.

The apostle Paul, strong as he was, a Pharisee of the Pharisees, had a problem with his will. He described it in Romans 7:18 when he said, "To will is present with me; but how to perform that which is good I find not." Paul had discovered a mighty principle of human nature, that there is more to following the will of God than simply making a right choice. The word *will* in this connection refers to the power of choice. Paul found that he could choose the right things, make the right decisions, but that it was impossible for him to follow through. Perhaps the same problem was what caused King Saul to be so weak and spineless. He would occasionally find the desire to do right, but when he tried to follow through on that desire, he didn't have the strength to perform.

But Philippians 2:13 tells us an amazing thing about the will, or the power of decision or choice. God, who works within us, wants to do *both* the willing and the doing. He is eager not only to show us the right choice to make, but to make the right choice in us, and then give us the power to do that which He has chosen for us.

Does that sound scary? Does it sound like heresy? Notice the words of Joshua there at the Jordan River. He didn't say, "Choose you this day what you will do." He said, "Choose . . . *whom ye will serve*." Another way of saying it might be, "Choose whose servant you will become."

Think for a moment about the master/servant relationship. Who chooses what the servant is going to do? The master or the servant? Who chooses what the servant is going to *choose*? The master or the servant? The servant has one choice, really. His choice is whether or not to remain a servant. Once that decision is made, it is the master who makes the decisions, not the servant.

Jesus often used the analogy of the servant/master relationship in His attempt to explain the workings of our relationship with God and the laws of the kingdom of heaven. He spoke of the servants to whom the master gave certain talents, to one five talents, to another two talents, and to a third only a single talent. He spoke of the unfaithful servants who killed the vineyard owner's messengers, and in the end even killed the heir himself. He told of the servants who were sent out to find guests for the feast prepared by the king. He spoke of the servants who did not know at what hour their master would return and so had to always be ready for his coming. And in the Sermon on the Mount He presented a universal and timeless principle: that no servant can serve more than one master. "No man can serve two masters: for either he will hate the one, and love the other; or else he will hold to the one, and despise the other." Matthew 6:24.

Why is it impossible for one servant to serve two masters? Because the choices the masters would make for that servant would conflict. A servant cannot serve two masters because it is impossible to surrender one's power of choice to more than one authority at one time. You cannot be under the control of General Motors and the Chrysler Corporation simultaneously. There is a term for what happens when someone tries to be loyal to two opposing forces at once. It's called "conflict of interest." And to have a conflict of interest is, in most cases, sufficient grounds for termination of employment. No man can serve two masters.

It is not possible to be a citizen of the United States and of the Soviet Union at the same time. Dual citizenship is possible only for children who have been born abroad, and when they reach adulthood they have a decision to make.

No citizen can serve two countries.

It is not possible to be controlled by God and by any other power at the same time. There are only two powers, when it comes to the control of the human being. It's either God or the devil. There is no third option. Throughout the Bible, there are two groups described. They have many labels: the sheep and the goats, the wise and the foolish, the righteous and the wicked, the wheat and the tares. Only in Revelation 3 do we find a middle group: the lukewarm, and the lukewarm are not given very good marks in Scripture. In fact, God, goes so far as to say that He would prefer that they were cold. Lukewarm is *worse* than cold. Trying to straddle the fence is worse than being on the wrong side of the fence! If you are on the wrong side of the fence, you may have hope of changing your mind. But if you've never made up your mind in the first place, you are in a dangerous position indeed. And it isn't long before the lukewarm are forced to go either hot or cold. There is no lukewarm lake of fire for the lukewarm!

Does the idea of control by God seem strange and frightening? Haven't you sung the song which one radio preacher described as "the song nobody means"? It's called, "Have Thine Own Way, Lord." Do you remember the words?

Have Thine own way, Lord! Have Thine own way!
Thou art the Potter; I am the clay.
Mold me and make me after Thy will,
While I am waiting, yielded and still.

Have Thine own way, Lord! Have Thine own way!
Hold o'er my being absolute sway!
Fill with Thy Spirit till all shall see
Christ only, always, living in me!

Is that a good song, or is that a song that should never be sung? It's a song about complete control by God.

Paul takes up the analogy of the master/servant relationship in Romans 6:16, where he says, "Know ye not, that to whom ye yield yourselves servants to obey, his servants ye are to whom ye obey; whether of sin unto death, or of obedience unto righteousness?" We have no choice in this world about whether we are going to be controlled. The only choice we have is about who will control us. We either serve sin, or we serve righteousness. It's either one or the other.

How do we make the choice as to whether God or the devil will control us? How do we make the choice as to which of the two great powers will be the ruling power in our lives? It is through coming into relationship with God, or refusing that relationship with Him. It is not necessary to choose against God. All that is required to refuse His control is not to choose *for* Him. The result of not choosing the control of God is automatic. Matthew 12:30 says it, recording the words of Jesus Himself on the subject: "He that is not with me is against me; and he that gathereth not with me scattereth abroad."

Once again we have come to the bottom line in all of knowing God's will, in all of understanding guidance from above. In order to know God's will, we must know God. The personal, vital, daily relationship with Him is what makes it possible, not only to know that which is good, but also to find the power and grace from above to perform it. It is only through coming to Him day by day, spending time in His Word, in the study of His life and character, in beholding Him, and in communing with Him through prayer, that we come under His control. Apart from that relationship with Him, it is pointless to even try to consider knowing God's will in our lives, for apart from His control, apart from His Spirit working in us, we will miss it either on the willing or on the doing or both. Every time.

But as we live in fellowship with Him, the decisions of life that are presented to us can be decided by Him who loves us and knows what is for our best interest. What an assurance this can bring to the heart when the time comes to *make a decision.*

Step 8
God's Will and the Swinging Doors

As we come to this final step in seeking to know God's will in your life, it might be meaningful to take just a few moments to review the steps so far, by way of summary:

1. Have no will of your own on the given matter.
2. Don't go by feelings.
3. Consult God's Word, both for information and communication.
4. Consider providential circumstances.
5. Consult your godly friends.
6. Pray about the decision.
7. Make a decision, and tell God what decision you have made, based on the evidence gathered in the preceding steps.
8. And now, *Proceed with your decision*, being sensitive to the swinging doors. Go ahead as if you have made the correct decision, but invite God to stop you if you have missed your signals for any reason.

This last step can be exciting, because it gives you an opportunity to watch God at work in your life. It can also be frustrating if you have somehow made a wrong decision. But you will discover, as many have discovered before you, that God is an expert at handling the doors.

Let's go first to the book of Revelation, the third chapter. We're not interested in doing an exposition on this passage in Revelation 3, in the message to the church of Philadelphia. There have been any number of prophetic and historic interpretations of these verses, some of which have proven incorrect, and some not. But we want to notice just one point, from verses 7 and 8:

"To the angel of the church in Philadelphia write; These things saith he that is holy, he that is true, he that hath the key of David, he that openeth, and no man shutteth; and shutteth, and no man openeth; I know thy works: behold, I have set before thee an open door, and no man can shut it; for thou hast a little strength, and hast kept my word, and hast not denied my name."

Whatever else these verses may refer to, one point is clear: God knows how to open and shut doors. If God opens a door, no man can shut it. And if God shuts a door, no man has the power to open it.

But you may wonder, after studying these eight steps, "How can I know that God is in control of the doors?" "What if I think I've made a right decision, but the doors seem to close in our way—couldn't it be the devil trying to discourage me?" "Does the devil have any control over the doors?" These are practical questions, for if we are seeking to know the will of God, we must be able to trust Him with the doors.

As with every other step, the first thing to underscore is the absolute necessity of the ongoing personal relationship with God day by day, in order to be under His control even before seeking to know His will on a given decision. The greatest safeguard against being led astray by any of the devices of the enemy is to know God for yourself, so that you can distinguish His voice from the voice of a stranger.

But does God always cause the doors to open spontaneously and immediately when we are following His voice? Are we guaranteed that everything will quickly "fall into place" when we have understood His guidance correctly? Do the doors ever appear to close for a time, but open in the end, at the direction of God Himself?

To our human understanding, it seems like the doors ought to open right away, unless we have missed our signals. I wish I could assure you that if you have followed these eight steps carefully and made a decision that is in harmony with the will of God, the doors will always open wide, and stay open; that if the doors seem to close in your face, you can know that somehow you have made a wrong decision. I wish I could assure you of that, but the Bible has a different story to tell! If we are going to be faithful to the Bible record, we discover that doors can be very tricky and stubborn things!

It is no more possible to depend upon step eight, the opening and closing of doors, as the final word on God's will for your life, than it is to depend upon any other single step alone. If the open and closed doors provided full and final proof of the will of God, then we could safely bypass all the other steps in knowing God's will and simply depend on telling God we're headed in a particular direction unless He stops us. We'd know that unless we were stopped, we were in harmony with His will.

There is no more safety in depending solely upon the opening and closing doors than there is in going by your own feelings or in depending upon what your family or friends tell you is the right decision.

If you make your way through the eight steps for knowing God's will in your life and then find in the end that the doors are apparently shut in your face, of course you will want to go back and seriously reconsider your decision. You will want to regroup, review, rethink your position. But frustrating as it is, the Bible precedent is that there may be times when God's will is for you to go forward, even though for a time He makes it appear impossible for you to do so!

Let's consider several Bible biographies as we try to understand this principle—perhaps the hardest principle to understand in all of Christian living—the *waiting* principle.

Adam is at the head of the line! After being found by God there in the Garden, hiding among the fig leaves, he was given a promise. The Messiah was going to come. Through the coming Saviour, forgiveness for his sin would be possible, and restoration to the lost Eden would be assured. When his first child was born, Adam was sure this must be the promised Son. If Cain wasn't the One, then surely Abel, who lingered at the altar morning and evening and seemed so sensitive to spiritual things. But Cain turned out to be a murderer—and Abel was his victim. Adam then pinned his hopes on Seth, and perhaps upon every succeeding son and grandson and great-grandson, until the end of his life. The promise had been given, God's will was clear. But Adam had to wait.

Noah had problems with the opening and closing doors! He thought he understood the guidance of God in beginning construction on an ark. For 120 years he hammered and preached and waited. Many who were convicted by his startling message at the beginning of the 120 years had stopped being convicted by the time more than a century had passed by. They were sure that Noah had missed his signals completely. During that time, Noah surely had opportunity to go back and reconsider the events that had led him to believe that God had directed him in the building of this boat. One hundred twenty years is a long time! And as if that were not enough, even after the animals had gathered from field and forest and Noah and his family had boarded the boat, they still had to wait awhile longer. God shut the door—and no man could open it! But it was still another seven days before the rain began. Then it rained for forty days and nights—followed by more than a year of waiting for the flood waters to dry up and the door to open, so they could escape from the boat that had been both a haven and a prison! Noah certainly knew what it meant to wait.

Abraham waited. Twenty-five years passed from the time he was first given the promise of a son. He tried to help God out by offering to take his servant as an heir, and then by his marriage to Hagar, but all of his efforts to find a shortcut were of no avail. They only caused problems in the end. Abraham had not misunderstood God's will. He had only misunderstood God's timetable.

Jacob was promised the birthright, as we noticed earlier. He, too, tried to hurry things along by helping God out. He hadn't been wrong in deciding that it was God's will for him to have the birthright, but he certainly wasn't prepared for the more than thirty years he had to wait before the promise was fulfilled.

Moses recognized the hand of God in his life when he was given the assignment of leading the people of Israel out of the land of Egypt. It didn't seem to him that the doors were opening quickly enough, and so he tried to hurry things along. Then it looked like the door was closed completely for forty years while he lived in the desert and herded his father-in-law's sheep. But there came a day when he reached the burning bush, and once again it seemed the doors were opening before him.

After arguing the matter at some length, Moses finally submitted to the plan of God for his life and went down to Egypt. But even then, his expectations were seldom met. He had hardly arrived in Egypt before Pharaoh received word of his mission and began to put the pressure on. The people came and complained to Moses—and Moses went to the Lord with a plaintive and almost funny prayer. You can read it in Exodus 5:23, where he said, "Since I came to Pharaoh to speak in thy name, he hath done evil to this people; neither hast thou delivered thy people *at all*."

Moses struggled with the doors. The people of Israel struggled with the doors. After every plague that came, it looked like the doors were opening—but after every deliverance from a plague, the doors slammed shut again. After the last plague and the slaying of the firstborn of Egypt, the doors seemed to open—but a few days later on the banks of the Red Sea, the doors seemed to shut. Then they opened again, as the people walked across on dry land!

It took only a couple of years to reach the borders of the Promised Land the first time, but then the people shut the doors in their own faces and had to wait thirty-eight years before the doors could open again. It makes you weary just reading about it!

What about Joseph? He had dreams. Were the dreams from God? Absolutely! Did they come true? They certainly did. But there were a few complications along the way—like exile and slavery and imprisonment and more than twenty years of waiting for the doors to finally open. But when the doors opened, they opened wide.

David was brought in from herding sheep in the mountains and fields. He was anointed King of Israel, much to his surprise and the surprise of his family. But it took many years for him to actually reach the throne—and for the entire time he seemed to be getting progressively further away from ever realizing the fulfillment of the promises he had been given. There were a lot of closed doors for David.

Do you find it depressing to look over the list of people who had to wait, sometimes years, for the doors to open? Or do you find it reassuring, as you try to come to terms with the unfinished business in your own life? Whatever feelings you may have, as you consider those who have waited for the doors to open, you have to admit that it happens so often as to be almost the rule rather than the exception!

Hebrews 11:39 makes record of those who died, never having received the things promised, having only seen them from afar—yet they still died in the faith. They followed the guidance of God in their lives, as far as they were able to follow, but the doors only opened so far, and the end of their lives found them still waiting.

There was a poem given at my graduation by H. M. S. Richards, the radio pastor, who was the speaker on that occasion.

> Now Adam said to Seth his son,
> When Adam's life was nearly done,
> I'm the first man that e're was made
> And yet a failure, I'm afraid.
> But you are young and life is thine.
> You'll have a chance that ne're was mine
> When I at last give up the fight.
> Go in there—make the old thing right.
>
> Centuries came, and centuries fled,
> And Seth called Enos near, and said,
> I've failed to do my father's word
> And always, ever serve the Lord.
> But you are young, and life's before;

Take up the flickering torch I bore
When I at last am passed from sight.
Go in there—make the old thing right.

But Enos, when the years had gone,
Passed still the self-same burden on,
And his son passed it on to others—
These others yet to other others.
To son and grandson, on again
And on, and on to other men.
The call still came from Eden's night
Go in there—make the old thing right.

And still it rings through all our years
Mid war and peace, in smiles and tears.
The call comes down again, again,
The anguished cry of troubled men
Who try the ancient course to run
And do their work e're set of sun.
But still they call, as falls the night,
Go in there—make the old thing right.

So folks today, let's rise and shine;
The best of all the years are thine.
Do now the task, e're set of sun
That others of them might have done.
Go where God calls; His word proclaim
For loving service, not for fame.
In Christ find courage, hope and light.
Go in there—make the old thing right.

There may be times when you have followed through
the steps for knowing God's will in your life and have
missed your signals. When that happens, most often the

mistake was made on the first step. Most often we fail in coming to the place of having no will of our own on the given matter. But there may be other times when you have followed through the steps, and have made a right decision, but you still have to wait for the doors to open. It's frustrating. It's scary. It's exciting. And it's also par for the course in the Christian life!

Why are there delays? Why is it that we so often must wait and wait and wait? It's because God, in all the guidance that He offers to His children, has more at stake than the immediate crisis or decision. He has our character development to consider. He sees the whole pattern of our lives for Him, not just the one isolated choice. And He has the plans and purposes that He is working for the entire universe at stake in the lives of His people.

We often come to Him seeking some blessing, and if He responds by answering our prayers with the blessing we request, we are content and conclude that our faith in Him is great. But the real test of our faith comes when there is a delay. What happens then? Do we give up, concluding that whatever we were seeking at His hand is not worth waiting for? Do we give up our relationship with Him when He does not meet our expectations? Or do we continue to seek Him, regardless of where He leads or how He leads or when He leads?

One reason why the doors open slowly is that God has something better for us. He not only wants to give us the guidance and blessing that we seek, but He wants to help us to grow as well, to develop a greater trust in Him and in His wisdom and power.

When God puts you "on hold," do you hang up? Or do you hang on? Are you willing to wait as long as is necessary—even if your waiting overlaps into eternity—rather than go outside of His will for you? Does it seem that you have been waiting a long time for some of the doors in your life to open and let you through? Don't look on the waiting time as time that is lost. The waiting itself is all part of the process by which God works to guide you, to perfect you, and to prepare you for the work He has assigned you.

We've spent a lot of time considering the doors that open slowly—but there's good news! Sometimes the doors open right away! That's an easier truth to accept, isn't it? And it is also truth, just as it is true that often the doors do *not* open immediately!

Elijah didn't have to wait for the fire to come down from heaven when he prayed on Mount Carmel. It fell from heaven right then. David didn't have to wait for help with his slingshot when Goliath came to meet him. Daniel didn't have to wait for deliverance from the mouths of the lions, and his three friends didn't have to wait for God to cool the fires of the furnace in their behalf.

Let's read one account of the doors opening quickly that is recorded in Acts 16. Paul and his companions had been preaching the gospel, traveling from one place to another. Verses 6-10 say: "Now when they had gone throughout Phrygia and the region of Galatia, and were forbidden of the Holy Ghost to preach the word in Asia, after they were come to Mysia, they assayed to go into Bithynia: but the Spirit suffered them not. And they passing by Mysia came down to Troas. And a vision appeared to Paul in the night; There stood a man of Macedonia, and prayed him, saying, Come over into Macedonia, and help us. And after he had seen the vision, immediately we endeavoured to go into Macedonia, assuredly gathering that the Lord had called us for to preach the gospel unto them."

Within a very short time, Paul was met with a closed door to Asia, a closed door to Bithynia, and then a wide-open door to Macedonia. He didn't have to wait 120 years or forty or seven. The guidance for his work came right away, just when it was needed.

As you seek to know the will of God in your own life, there will be times of both: times when you will have to wait, and times when the answer will come overnight. And we can be thankful for both, for both open and closed doors are part of God's method for giving us His guidance in our lives. We can gain many insights into God's will in our lives by watching the swinging doors.

We can afford to make a lot of mistakes when it comes to decision making, which is good news, because many of us have made a lot of mistakes! But there is one mistake we cannot afford to make, and that is to stop praying and seeking to know God for ourselves, that we may be in such close relationship with Him that we will recognize His guidance. As we continue to come to Him, He has given us the promise of communicating to us, not only His will for our lives, but the knowledge of Himself, whom to know is life eternal.